CLIMATES OF THE MIND

A Bipolar Memory
Including the Therapy Journals

Jerry Jewler

iUniverse, Inc.
Bloomington

Climates of the Mind
A Bipolar Memory Including the Therapy Journals

Copyright © 2009 Jerry Jewler

iUniverse books may be ordered through booksellers or by contacting:

iUniverse
1663 Liberty Drive
Bloomington, IN 47403
www.iuniverse.com
1-800-Authors (1-800-288-4677)

ISBN: 978-1-4401-9350-7 (pbk)
ISBN: 978-1-4401-9348-4 (cloth)
ISBN: 978-1-4401-9349-1 (ebook)

Printed in the United States of America

iUniverse rev. date: 12/30/09

I dedicate this book to my loving family. To Belle, my wife of nearly fifty years, to our children, Melissa Welsh and Scott Jewler, and to our adorable granddaughters, Lena and Kay Jewler. I also dedicate this work to the many other wonderful friends and family who have helped shape my life for the better.

Contents

About the Author ix
Introduction xi

Chapter 1:   Drifting 1
Chapter 2:   What If? 3
Chapter 3:   What Might Have Been 6
Chapter 4:   Stargazing 9

THE THERAPY JOURNALS: 1995 11

Chapter 5:   Smart Little Devil 23
Chapter 6:   Seeking the Source 28
Chapter 7:   Sarah 32
Chapter 8:   Life after Sarah 37
Chapter 9:   An Awful Adolescence 40

THE THERAPY JOURNALS: 1996–97 49

Chapter 10: Army Times 56
Chapter 11: Mommas 67
Chapter 12: Heartsick 74
Chapter 13: Luke 77
Chapter 14: Learning from Learners 81
Chapter 15: Brokenhearted 86

THE THERAPY JOURNALS: 2008–9 93

Chapter 16: Hard Times 103
Chapter 17: Faith in Myself 108
Chapter 18: The Best of Friends 112
Chapter 19: A Temporary Setback 116
Chapter 20: Another Teaching Turn 118
Chapter 21: Adding Things Up 121

About the Author

By the time I turned sixty in 1995, I had established myself as a popular professor of mass communications at the University of South Carolina for twenty-three years, and had collaborated in writing two highly successful series of college textbooks which have been in print since the early 1980s. I wanted to celebrate my "coming of age" that year with a splashy party, and Belle, my wife, planned and hosted a lollapalooza of an evening. The next morning, I awakened to a hell I had never known.

This marked the beginning of a regimen of therapy sessions and medications that I continue to this day. My earliest visits to a psychiatrist confirmed that I was bipolar, had been bipolar all my life, and would require therapy and medicine for this disorder for the rest of my life. In writing this book, I have attempted to share parts of my life and the insights I have gained about my condition. In contemplating the source of my mental state, I ultimately concluded that my beloved paternal grandmother, Sarah Jewler, may have been the one who passed those unfortunate genes down to me. Baba Sarah, as I called her, was not only the focus of my earliest days, but a person to be reckoned with during her entire life. Although my memories and insights frequently jump back and back and forth in time, it's simply how my mind works. Nonetheless, readers should have no trouble following my personal journey of self-discovery and learning how to cope.

When I retired in 2000, I began a vigorous search for volunteer work that would complement my talents and experiences, culled from years of writing and college teaching. Without a structured schedule after more than forty years of steady work, I feared that my bipolar disorder would only worsen. Luckily I found my calling at the South Carolina State Museum, where I have conducted tours for school groups and adults since 2002. More recently, I accepted a volunteer position at the information desk of the Richland County Public Library in Columbia, South Carolina, where we have lived since 1972. Our grown son and daughter have distinguished themselves in careers that were a perfect match for their talents and temperaments. We are rightly proud of them, and of our two bright granddaughters, Kay and Lena, whose mother is Japanese.

An avid film buff, I own a collection of more than three hundred movies, many from the "golden age" of Hollywood, as well as a modest library of books about the movies.

I had a brief stint in community theater some years ago, appearing in half a dozen plays, including *Six Degrees of Separation*, in which I was cast as the male lead. It was another way to forget who I was and become somebody else, if only for a few hours each evening.

Born in Washington DC, I eventually moved to the surrounding Maryland suburbs and lived there until 1958, the year I was drafted into the Army to serve at Fort Jackson, South Carolina, where I met and fell in love with Belle. When she and I were married in 1960, we spent eight hapless years in the Washington area before returning to the South we both love— first to Charlotte, North Carolina, later to Greenville, South Carolina, and ultimately back to Columbia, Belle's hometown and the city I call home..

Introduction

Although my behavior since early childhood might have raised suspicions, I was not diagnosed with bipolar disorder until my sixtieth birthday. Until then, I believed that my frequent and inexplicable mood swings were par for the course. As far as I knew, no one in my family took my frequent rants seriously and most likely, they were unaware of my occasional periods of depression. I suspect they figured I'd grow up and out of my "temper tantrums" soon enough.

In the 1930s and '40s, the term "bipolar disorder" had not yet been coined, and would not enter the language for decades. For hundreds of years, scientists had treated mental patients for "mania," "depression," "melancholy," and even "circular insanity," eventually discovering that mood disorders were genetic in origin. In 1980, the term "bipolar disorder" replaced "manic-depressive disorder" as a diagnostic term in the *Diagnostic and Statistical Manual* of the American Psychiatric Association.

I experienced one of my first major mood swings during the summer following my graduation from junior high, when my family moved from Washington DC to suburban Silver Spring, Maryland. Although only ten miles or so from our old neighborhood, it might as well have been in another country as far as I was concerned. With his income falling and his health failing, Dad grabbed at an opportunity to share ownership in a new supermarket in the burgeoning suburbs. We moved from our row house in northwest Washington, where I had lived since I was four, to an apartment within walking distance of the new store. Mom, who wasn't driving yet, made the short walk to the store each day to cashier.

The market was the only one in a new residential area and business was steady, but all that mattered to me was that my dream of following my junior high classmates to Roosevelt High in DC had evaporated. Throughout the summer, I pleaded in vain to be allowed to live with my grandmother, so I would be eligible to join my friends that fall. My parents wouldn't hear of it, and that summer became a silent and torturous one for us all. I rarely spoke to my parents and, even worse, spent hours sprawled on the sofa with my head buried in a pillow as they went about their business. I sighed and moaned to no avail. I was miserable and wanted my family to understand that. If I could drive them bananas with my behavior, perhaps they would change their minds. The idea of having a heart-to-heart talk didn't occur to me—or to them. One Sunday afternoon, Dad told Mom to take my sister, Roberta, for a walk, and to stay out for at least an hour. Alone with me in the apartment, he demanded to know why I was acting so strangely. I clammed up. I figured that I already had given him plenty of clues, so why bother explaining. Demanding an answer, he chased me from room to room. I remember screaming when Mom and Roberta walked in. Horrified by what she saw and heard, Mom put her foot down, which was quite out of character for her, and told Dad to quit bothering me. I felt a small glow of warmth in knowing that at least she was concerned, even though nothing really had changed.

In September, feeling like a fish out of water, I began attending Montgomery Blair High School. By my sophomore year, my circle of friends had improved and with it, my disposition. In my senior year, Dad died of cancer at the age of forty-one. Though I sensed that we were standing on shaky ground, I was more concerned about Mom's survival than about the death of my father. Mom seemed so helpless that I felt it was my duty to take charge. When Mom used the proceeds from Dad's small life insurance policy to lease a candy business in Silver Spring, I promised I would help her make the store a success. Before long, I was telling her how to run the business and bugging the hell out of her.

That fall, I began my freshman year as a commuter student at the University of Maryland in College Park. Before the academic year was over, I threatened to quit because I found running the candy shop far more interesting than attending classes. Of all people, it was my grandmother who insisted I stay in college, and this time I listened. How different my life would have been had I dropped out!

In college, I began to recognize how petulant I could be one moment, and how wildly happy the next. I thought this was a normal part of my personality. In those days, most folks believed that psychiatrists treated crazy people, and I wasn't crazy by any means.

And so I survived adolescence, fulfilled my two-year military obligation, fell in love and married, had two children, and drifted from the advertising business into higher education.

More and more, my extreme mood swings were greatly diminishing my ability to enjoy life and to act in a rational manner. I would blurt out words without first considering their consequences. Though I loved them all, Belle and the children were forever getting on my nerves. I was beginning to hate my work, question my professional abilities, and shy away from large groups of people. In desperation, I called our family physician, who asked if I would agree to psychiatric therapy. His referral laid the groundwork for the diagnosis that helped me to survive. Since then, I have learned a great deal about the reasons for my erratic behavior.

The exact cause of bipolar disorder has not been discovered, but many experts believe that multiple factors may contribute to the condition. My therapist was careful to define my mental state in terms I could understand. He began by explaining that a chemical called serotonin, a neurotransmitter, connects the cells of the brain by sending electrical charges between them, so the brain can make meaningful and logical connections. When serotonin levels are fairly constant, the result is clarity of thought.

In the brain of a person who has the bipolar gene, however, serotonin levels tend to rise and fall in unexpected patterns. When they fall precipitously, the brain begins to lose focus and finds it difficult to perform the most basic tasks, since the links between brain cells have begun to fade. My therapist compared this state to a brownout in a town's electrical system. In the human brain, the faulty circuits lead to confusion and depression.

At this point, the adrenal glands, sensing the low serotonin levels in the brain, rush to the rescue by pumping huge amounts of adrenalin to the brain to raise serotonin levels. With just the right amount of adrenalin, the individual will feel energized but calm. But when the adrenals overcompensate, the brain is besieged with anxiety, panic, and mania. The sudden "rush" felt by the individual ultimately overloads the circuits, resulting in paranoia, feelings of worthlessness, and a recycling into another period of depression as serotonin levels drop once more.

The cycle repeats itself endlessly in a catch-22 bipolar nightmare.

Some cycles may last days, weeks, or months, or the individual might experience ups and downs several times in a single day.

What are bipolar individuals likely to think or feel?

- I'm both bored and boring.
- You never want to do anything with me.
- What is the point of life?
- Why can't I make friends with anyone?
- I'm just not up to the task anymore.
- I wish I were dead.

- I always knew I was a failure. All my achievements were merely a façade.
- I am so embarrassed about my stupidity.
- I cry so easily.
- I can't cry at all.
- Is this all there is?
- I'll never be creative again. I've run dry.
- I wake up each morning and wish I could just stay in bed.
- I feel tremendous guilt.
- I often take things the wrong way.
- I am sensitive to what others say about me.
- I have such great plans, but can't seem to get started on anything.
- I'll do anything to avoid work.
- Someone is always doing something better than I can.

Many individuals with mental disorders are too embarrassed or frightened to seek help, or simply don't realize they need help. Now I realize the importance of therapy, of having the opportunity to describe your feelings to a psychiatrist. It is empowering to be able to explain your condition to others without fear or embarrassment.

In fact, I strongly believe that being able to grasp the nature of the problem and to feel comfortable explaining it to others can help remove the stigma and embarrassment normally associated with mental disorders, not only for the patient, but for others as well.

CHAPTER 1

Drifting

Throughout the inky night, blasts of icy wind chill me to the bone. I am gazing through the plate-glass window of a dazzlingly bright shop jammed with happy folks who flit from aisle to aisle, grabbing packages from the shelves. Though their sizes and shapes are different, each package is already gift wrapped in gleaming golden foil and tied with a glittery golden ribbon and frilly bow.

Even though a thick sheet of plate glass separates us, I can see and hear the frivolity inside. People laugh and chat, help one another reach for packages from the taller shelves, smile, schmooze, and keep shopping. No one is checking out; it's as if they don't want to leave the store, and I don't blame them.

Pushing the door open, I enter the store. It's so cozy in here that I feel smothered by my wool topcoat, flannel scarf, and winter hat. I unbutton the coat and begin to slip the sleeves from my arms. As I do, my elbows bump into something hard, and I realize that I am encased in a transparent cylinder. My joy turns to anxiety, but thankfully, it is short lived. The cylinder vanishes, and I am at last mingling with those happy shoppers, who beckon me to join them in their gala shopping spree. I am so happy! I smile. I chat. Then, as quickly as it began, my happiness fades, and I am overwhelmed by all the commotion around me.

I try to speak, but words fail me. As I move forward, the crowd peels away on either side, like Moses parting the Red Sea. Seemingly oblivious of my presence, the people keep chatting with each other as if I were not there. I feel a great urge to escape, but I do not see any doors or windows. At that precise moment of ultimate panic, I emit a bloodcurdling scream and awaken, drenched in sweat.

CHAPTER 2

What If?

Though I accept that I might have been a happier person were it not for my bipolar disorder, I wonder if I could have accomplished so much, had I been born without it.

On the day of my bar mitzvah, I might not have scolded my aunt for rearranging the food at the reception following the ceremony. I might have avoided the deep depression I experienced when I learned we would be moving to the Maryland suburbs because I wanted so badly to follow my junior high friends in Washington DC to high school. I might never have threatened to drop out of college during my freshman year.

Once, during a job interview, I was chided for seeking a position that "was beneath the dignity of a person with two college degrees." Leaving that office, I began to lose not only my sense of confidence, but also my hope of ever finding a job. For what seemed like ages, I felt like a loner and a loser. My marriage became a series of alternating moments of deep love and unrelenting tension. Even when I was hired as a college professor, I allowed a colleague to denigrate me every chance he got and believed he was the smarter one and I the fool. I feared failure constantly, although I was lauded repeatedly as a great teacher, advisor, and leader, and had garnered a number of professional awards.

Might it all have been different? Watching the movie version of Patricia Highsmith's novel *The Talented Mr. Ripley* for the third or fourth time, I suddenly wondered why I felt a strange connection to the story. At the end of the film, I switched to the interviews on the DVD, and listened to actor Matt Damon explaining that he was intrigued with playing Ripley because the character is a young man stuck in a dead-end career as a piano accompanist and has the ambition, but lacks the means, to rise higher.

By a twist of fate, Ripley escapes his humdrum life by emulating a rich playboy, eventually murdering him and taking his place. In Ripley, I recognized the desire of many of us to rise above our stations, to toss away our desolate selves and gain the chance to enjoy a better life. The tag line for the Ripley film reads, "How far would you go to become someone else?"

Unlike Ripley, I would hardly kill for such "rewards," but during my youth and at various other times in my life, I frequently wished I were anyone but the inept individual I believed myself to be.

In Alfred Hitchcock's film version of another Highsmith novel, *Strangers on a Train*, a twisted young man named Bruno meets a handsome tennis player, Guy, and eerily jokes about "exchanging murders" with him. Guy views Bruno's scheme as pure nonsense, and he is horrified to discover that Bruno actually has murdered Guy's estranged wife so that Guy can marry his fiancée, and asks Guy to carry out his part of the deal by killing the father that Bruno detests.

In *Ripley*, the transformation actually occurs, while in *Strangers,* the act of strangling another man's wife provides the killer with an entrée into the glamorous social life of the well-known tennis player he so admires. Both movies have characters who, like me, wanted to live different lives.

Bipolar disorder, I have learned, is largely an inherited condition that includes such manic symptoms as feelings of euphoria, rapid speech, racing thoughts, taking chances, a tendency to be easily distracted, and aggressive behavior. In the depressive phase, sufferers feel sadness, anxiety, guilt, and hopelessness; exhaustion and loss of interest in daily activities; problems concentrating and irritability; and chronic pain without a known cause. One can have manic and depressive feelings at the same time, or they may cycle back and forth. When I sense a downer coming on, I try, often in vain, to remind myself that it isn't a permanent state of mind. In a manic mood, I plummet from happiness to an overwhelming anxiety as I fight to cope with my racing thoughts and actions.

Since adolescence, I've frequently experienced a sort of claustrophobia when I find myself in a crowded room, where everyone is engaged in conversation except me. As a result, I developed a habit of fixing my gaze at the ceiling, believing that, if I couldn't see them, perhaps they couldn't see me standing there looking awkward. Even when a friend joked, "What in hell is so interesting up there?" I continued this behavior as a way to escape one of my profoundest fears. My cousin, who is a physician, suggested this behavior might indicate another condition called Asperger's Syndrome, which occasionally coexists with bipolar disorder. As he described Asperger's, I began to suspect he might be right, although I have never been diagnosed with the condition. Asperger's symptoms include the inability or a lack of desire to interact with peers, a poor appreciation of social cues, limited interests, repetitive routines, misinterpretation of literal and implied meanings of others, a peculiar stiff gaze, and motor clumsiness.

So much of that fits me like a glove.

CHAPTER 3

What Might Have Been

Watching a PBS documentary on choreographer Jerome Robbins, I became fascinated with the parallels as well as the major differences in our lives. Robbins had also grown up in a Jewish family and was dragged along to dancing school with his sister, just as I was. Born and raised in New York City, Robbins chose dancing as a career and subsequently achieved fame as a choreographer and director for stage and screen.

Reading a biography of Hollywood director Stanley Donen, I learned that he had abandoned his hometown (and my adopted one) of Columbia, South Carolina when he was sixteen, and had headed straight for Broadway. Starting as a chorus boy, he ultimately crossed paths with the legendary dancer-actor-choreographer-singer Gene Kelly, who was starring in *Pal Joey* on Broadway, and subsequently followed Kelly to Hollywood, where Kelly became an entertainer of the highest magnitude and Donen directed a string of sparkling Hollywood musicals, dramas, and comedies.

If it had happened to Robbins and Donen, why hadn't it happened to me? Since my grandmother had practically raised me on movies and vaudeville before I was old enough to begin school, I believed at that young, naïve age that by studying dancing and practicing my singing, I might one day attain fame and fortune in show business.

It was not to be. In junior high, I had acted in several plays. When my family moved to the suburbs just before my first year of high school, the resultant trauma I felt from being severed from my old friends caused me to stutter profoundly. Even so, I persisted in auditioning for a spring variety show at my new school. The audition was humiliating, and led me to wonder how I could ever have believed that theater was my calling when I could hardly spit out the words.

Much later, while living and teaching in Columbia, South Carolina, I decided to reconnect with the performing arts by signing up for a series of local acting classes. When my first acting teacher praised me for a soliloquy I presented in class and urged me to audition for a forthcoming local production of *The Night Thoreau Spent in Jail*, I felt the magic returning. Even though my part was tiny, simply being onstage proved thrilling, and I continued to read for parts and take additional classes. Eventually, I won a choice supporting role in a local production of *Born Yesterday* and later garnered a positive review as the gay uncle trying to smuggle his homosexual nephew out of Nazi Germany in Martin Sherman's brilliant play, *Bent*.

Then came the big one: a director cast me as the male lead in *Six Degrees of Separation*. My character was onstage throughout the show, and I had to make several lightning-quick changes in the wings. Thrilled as I was with my star turn, I began anxiously awaiting closing night as we began the second and final week of performances. Teaching by day and acting nightly was beginning to overwhelm me. After a bit part in another show, I went to a string of auditions without success. At that point, I felt the muse had abandoned me and gave up the stage for good.

Not long after, we received word that one of my wife Belle's close childhood friends was visiting Columbia with her eldest son and his family. Belle suggested we all meet for lunch at Harper's in Five Points.

Belle's friend was delightful and, along with her son, his wife, and their children, engaged in wonderful reminiscences of earlier times. Amidst the chatter in the noisy restaurant, her lovely daughter-in-law began recounting the amazing success story of one of her nephews. Bitten by the acting bug in high school, he had told his parents he was intent on show business and was damned serious about it. His parents must have looked at one another with dismay, but happily supported his dream, most likely believing that a dream was all there was to it.

But the boy persevered. He continued performing in college, where he majored in theater, took tap lessons followed by voice lessons, followed by more acting lessons, and ultimately found himself in a Broadway chorus. Now he's shooting for the big time and it seems as if nothing can stop him.

Thankfully, I no longer stutter, and I maintain my ties to local theater as a box office volunteer. Yet to this day, I allow myself to escape now and then to a world of fame and fortune in show business that might have been if somehow I had had the guts and talent to go for it.

---- CHAPTER 4 ----

Stargazing

As movies began to stand in for the more dismal realities of my life, I became especially taken with one star in particular. For those too young to remember, Judy Garland began her show business career as a young child and early on developed one of the greatest pop voices in history. At the age of seventeen, she achieved lasting fame as Dorothy in *The Wizard of Oz*. She followed that role with memorable film performances as Esther Smith *in Meet Me in St. Louis*, the vaudevillian who helps hoofer Gene Kelly find his heart in *For Me and My Gal*, the not-so-sharpshootin' waitress in *The Harvey Girls*, the sultry Manuela in *The Pirate*, and the effervescent Hannah Brown in *Easter Parade* with Fred Astaire.

A magical performer on stage and screen, in her real life she was burdened by her addiction to uppers and downers and an inability to manage the millions she earned. She died at forty-seven, worn out and broke.

Garland was not only a singer with an astounding and unique voice, but also a talented actor, dancer, and raconteur. Acquaintances recall that she was one of the wittiest people in the business. Not long after Belle and I were married, I opened *The Washington Post* one Sunday morning and found an ad announcing that Judy Garland was going to perform in person at Constitution Hall the following month. Though we were counting our pennies, I mailed a check first thing Monday morning for $12—big money for us in those days. Miraculously, we received two second-row center seats for the identical concert she would perform later that year at Carnegie Hall, the legendary two-disc recording of which is still available—and still selling.

Throughout the evening, I sat transfixed as Judy sang and delighted us with stories for two hours. Judy always had—and still has, years after her death—a large gay following, and we soon realized we were surrounded by gay men screaming "Bravo!" and "We love you, Judy!" after each song, which only added to the excitement of the evening. When she ended the performance with several encores, a flurry of spotlights crisscrossed the audience, making the stage shimmer as the vast crowd stood up and cheered for what seemed like an eternity. As Garland held out her hand to the audience, Belle was one of the many who reached for, and received, a handshake. Feeling an emotional wallop I had never felt before, I found it impossible to reach out and touch her.

Garland died of an accidental drug overdose in 1967. In 1983, after months of detective work, film historian Roland Haver was able to reconstruct her 1954 classic film, *A Star is Born*, to its original three-hour length. Viewing it on DVD for the first time, I felt the same elation I had felt more than twenty years earlier in Constitution Hall.

—— THE THERAPY JOURNALS: 1995 ——

As part of my therapy, I was told to jot down my thoughts and feelings as soon after each session as possible. The following journals were written between April and December 1995. During this initial phase of treatment, I would use these journals as scripts for our next session. As treatment progressed, I found less need to write before each meeting. I stopped writing altogether for a number of years, resuming with several more journals, stopping again, and once more resuming a regular schedule during a lengthy bad spell in 2009. I relied heavily on writing to express myself initially, but was able to speak more spontaneously as treatment progressed. Although some of the thoughts in the journals reappear in the narrative portion of this work, I've included them as historical records of what I was feeling at the time I was writing them.

April 21, 1995

To tell you the truth, I was nervous about our initial meeting, but you put my mind at rest. Imagine me needing a psychiatrist! I learned a great deal from you today about depression and panic, that both are produced by the sympathetic nervous system, over which we have no control. You reminded me about the "fight or flight" responses in primitive society which modern society must still contend with today. You also underscored that I should never shoulder the blame for feeling depressed, because my depression was being caused by a chemical imbalance that could be managed to a great degree through drugs and therapy.

I took your advice and asked my dean for a medical leave over the summer. She didn't hesitate to grant me one—with pay—for which I shall be forever grateful. Teaching, which I dearly love, has been hellish these last few months.

I still don't fully understand why I should be suffering this way and don't know if anyone can ever explain that. Maybe I wasn't listening closely enough during our session. When I came home, I took the .25 mg Xanax you prescribed. Had a drink before dinner and took another .50 mg dose at 10 PM, along with the Effexor (37.5 mg) and my usual medications for heart disease (Zocor, Verapamil, and aspirin). I fell asleep in the middle of one of my favorite television programs. When Belle poked me, I stood up, staggered toward the bedroom, downed the 50 mg of Trazadone that you prescribed to help me sleep, and slept soundly until 7 AM. After showering, I felt like getting back in bed, so I lay down and slept until ten.

By the weekend, much of the panic had subsided. While I wasn't exactly a barrel of laughs (far from it), that hollow, hopeless feeling was slowly fading.

After breakfast, I mowed the front lawn. It felt good to be working outdoors. I still doubt that my mind is clear enough for academic work, but I've chosen not to dwell on it. Instead of wondering whether I will ever be able to concentrate on anything again, I'm trying to use this time to relax and to appreciate the fact that I feel better. My former sadness is slowly turning into a feeling of relief.

I will continue writing this journal. It seems to help.

May 10, 1995

It's been only two weeks since our first session and already I'm handling tasks much better. Right now, I'm in the middle of grading final projects and feel elated at the quality of work my students have produced. Yet I long to wrap up the term and turn in my grades so that I can begin my summer break. Although I won't be teaching summer school, thanks to the kindness of my dean and the university, I'm conducting several one- or two-day out-of-town teaching workshops, which usually boost my self-esteem greatly. And there's more good news: I've resumed my swimming this week. During the first few laps, I became short of breath, but chalked it up to anxiety rather than heart trouble, since it began to dissipate quickly. Although I'm very relaxed these days, I don't feel drugged at all. In fact, my mind, if anything, seems sharper. Since I'm fairly exhausted by evening, I'm sleeping more soundly. The days seem to be flying by instead of feeling intolerably long and empty. I am enjoying the beautiful mornings again, and want this feeling to continue forever! Friends have been understanding and have noted positive changes in my behavior. Food even tastes so good that I am hungrier these days and crave things that should not be on my diet!

Yesterday we drove to Charlotte to attend a funeral. For the first time in ages—and considering the event—I can proudly report that I felt at ease among the crowd of mourners, most of whom I did not know, and chatted with a number of them instead of anxiously wishing I could escape. I no longer feel sad, anxious, or empty, nor am I hopeless or pessimistic. I am enjoying my leisure time immensely. Generally, I am amazed at my overall improvement, and most grateful to you for your guidance.

May 13, 1995

Several days ago, I conducted a workshop in Chattanooga. The workshop was designed to train faculty and staff to become more effective teachers through a humanistic approach. The workshop came off smoothly, but I don't think I could have done it without my current medications, despite having conducted nearly one hundred workshops before. One part of the training deals with group building and trust. Participants are asked to draw pictures of their lives and subsequently present them to the group. To get things rolling, I shared my current problems with depression and anxiety, not to evoke sympathy, but to help others understand bipolar disorder and to underscore that it was no disgrace to own a mental illness. After that session, a participant, who happened to be a psychology professor, walked up and thanked me for my candidness, adding that mental illness had been a taboo topic for too long. That gave me the confidence and energy I needed to continue, and by the time I dismissed the group, I was elated rather than exhausted, as I usually have been after the first day of a workshop.

After a relaxing weekend at home, I spent most of Monday in the office catching up on calls, meeting with graduate student project committees, and planning a new course I'll be team teaching next term. I suddenly felt wiped out around 2 PM, so I left early and drove home. I had not slept well over the weekend and was still tired when I awoke Tuesday morning, so I upped the Trazadone a bit that evening. My spirits, while better, are not great, but I'm definitely not depressed or panicky. Belle and I had a mild disagreement about replacing our luggage with a more expensive set, but we resolved that smoothly. Belle has periods of depression and is taking a mild antidepressant. Wonder if sometimes we unknowingly work at cross-purposes?

I discussed my bipolar disorder with my sole surviving aunt, Bette, who lives in suburban Maryland. She revealed that she had developed claustrophobia in her early twenties. About a year ago, upset by the death of a close relative, she was advised to take an antidepressant and said it helped greatly. It made me think: could there be some genetic basis for how I've been feeling? I was also reminded of her brother, my brilliant Uncle Jack, who was never able to find a meaningful career. An accomplished musician, and champion checkers player, he fell into a deep depression after coronary artery bypass surgery, and died a number of years ago.

May 30–June 14, 1995

For the time being at least, my exhaustion has dissipated and I feel so much better that I cut the Trazadone back to 50 mg at bedtime. I went to see a movie last night while Belle had a card game and, not surprisingly, felt some anxiety at first and was aware of tiny annoyances, such as light drifting in from the back of the auditorium and a continuous high-pitched hum. Finally, I relaxed and got into the film, which, while not great, was interesting. I swam three times this week and my endorphins kicked in, leaving me feeling happy and relaxed. Now that the spring term is over (hurrah!), Belle and I can begin packing for our trip to New Mexico. I finished reading the book you loaned me, *The Anxiety Disease*. While I found it hard to relate to all aspects, I found most of it enlightening.

We returned home from Santa Fe and agreed it was just about the best vacation of our lives, despite the fleeting depression I experienced toward the middle of the week. One evening, as I thought about the anxiety book and its claim that anxiety and other psychological disorders normally begin in one's late teen years, I began to recall events from that period in my life. My joyful childhood seemed to end when I was twelve with the death of Baba Sarah, my favorite grandmother. Fearful of going to her funeral, I was ordered by my grandfather to attend at the very last minute. This was the first funeral I had ever attended, and when I was told to approach the open casket and say good-bye, I was horrified to see the lifeless mask that had once been a vibrant face. For months, I looked under my bed every evening before going to sleep, fearing that her dead body was lying there. Four years later, my father died of cancer at the age of forty-one. I was seventeen. Those years, I now realize, marked the beginning of my descent into the predictable pattern of depression and mania.

May 31, 1995

I drove to Greensboro, about a three-hour trip, on Friday to conduct another workshop and blew a tire about ten miles from home. By the time I returned late Sunday evening, I was exhausted. On Monday morning, Belle's mother couldn't get her car started, so I drove over and got her going. I slept for nearly two hours that afternoon, and was still weary that night.

The workshop went well, but I was frustrated because I couldn't reach Belle by phone after many tries. By the time she answered, my frustration had left me stressed and irritable. Every now and then, I feel a slight shortness of breath, along with nausea, after completing some simple task, but the symptoms fade quickly. And, yes, I'm back to my old habit of worrying whether I've remembered to do everything on my list. I've also had the odd experience of wanting to relax but needing to work as well. I continue to catch up on my work in the comfort of my home office and drop by my college office once weekly to pick up mail and respond to phone messages. I find it difficult to stay there for long, but trust I'll be eager to resume work this fall. I still need to make some sense out of the new graduate seminar I'll be team-teaching this fall and have plenty of reading to do in preparation for it. Basically, I am most grateful for the good feelings I've experienced lately, and for the wonderful support from my family.

At home, Belle keeps the air conditioning at a level I regard as freezing! Sometimes I'm so cold in the house, I will put on a heavy robe to watch TV. Last night, after about an hour, I realized I was hot and removed the robe. Though generally serene these days, I still have some brief ups and downs, and frequently worry about how I'm going to fill some of my "empty days." Something in my life seems to be missing. Belle will be driving to Atlanta to visit Melissa this Friday. If the weather is nice, I may drive to Hunting Island and spend the day on that lovely, isolated beach.

Belle and I recently spent a pleasant afternoon together. We had lunch, went to a movie, and later wandered through the mall. Then she said something as we got into the car that really upset me and we rode home in silence. The following morning, we talked about it and both of us felt better. My mind jerks me around frequently these days: brief lows, brief highs, too tired to do anything. The nausea comes and goes. Despite it all, I resolved to drive to the fitness center today for a swim. Afterward, I felt fresh and alive, another reminder that it's always worth the time and effort, no matter how much I fight the idea, to keep up with my exercise program.

June 22, 1995

Perhaps I'm reading too much about depression. Yesterday, I surfed the Internet for "symptoms of depression" and spotted "nausea" and "abdominal distress," which naturally caused me to wonder if those symptoms were psychosomatic. Just before my swim today, I felt a slight dizziness, but it didn't seem to deter me as I swam my usual twelve laps. I also had another of those dull headaches this morning, along with some mild depression. I'm stuttering a bit more than usual—not constantly, but just enough to be annoying and embarrassing. This irritates and frustrates me, since I lived with a pronounced stutter for many years and was terrified of public speaking. This evening, as we were heading out for dinner, Belle said she didn't like riding with me because of my road rage. I promised to watch that, and appreciated that—for once—she was able to tell me what was bothering her instead of politely holding it in, which she agrees is not healthy for either of us.

Last Saturday I drove to Hunting Island and spent three glorious hours on the beach. On Sunday, I awoke with pain and swelling in my left elbow. Nonetheless, I managed to cut the grass, run errands, and relax. I spent a few hours reading page proofs for the latest edition of our textbook. Tonight, I'll be going to acting class. It's been years since I've studied acting, and I'm very anxious, even though I know most of the students and both of the teachers. In my heart, I know it will be fun—and that helps.

July 5, 1995

I haven't written much since I last saw you and discussed the nausea and dizziness I've frequently experienced. I followed your directions and stopped taking Effexor, then waited a couple of days before starting on the new antidepressant. I had to up my morning dosage of Xanax to .5 mg, but after a few days, I went back to the .25 mg dosage since the larger dose did nothing for the nausea. Since this weekend, my symptoms have become less pronounced and I'm actually feeling good. Occasionally, I get a touch of "swimmer's ear," so I'm using alcohol drops after swimming and showering. I wonder if this might be the reason for the dizzy spells. My neck and arms have felt so sore that I scheduled a massage for Monday, and it helped tremendously. Belle and I spent some time discussing how we bug each other. It was a frank, sensible, and helpful conversation.

Riding on a high, I drove to Chattanooga for another workshop on Wednesday and Thursday, and felt it went well. I had a graduate project defense Friday morning, after which I drove straight home and slept. Belle's ninety-two-year-old aunt fell and broke her hip yesterday and is having surgery this morning. We're both taking it calmly instead of allowing it to take over our lives. Progress, maybe?

I also discovered that, in the midst of this busy week, I had forgotten to take all of my heart medicines one evening. Could that account for some of my misery?

A few days have passed and it's Saturday again. I've been suffering from a rotten toothache for days and finally had the dentist check it. Last night, Belle and I went to two drop-ins and I tried to drown the agony of it all in gin. This morning I feel irritated and frustrated. I chided Belle last night about being on the phone so much. I was already grumpy and simply couldn't stand to listen to her long conversations any longer. She gave me hell and walked out of the room. I went back to sleep and awoke at 3 PM with the damned toothache again. The days have been painful, to say the least. On top of everything else, I had a confrontation with a female doctoral candidate who's been excusing herself from part of our seminar to "do her work for other faculty," which I discovered was a fabrication, for the most part. I hate confrontations of any sort, so I was totally wiped out after attempting to communicate my concerns, especially since she still believes that everyone's against her.

Even though I've had some downers lately, they seem to come and go, and I am managing to maintain a realistic perspective most of the time. I find that I stress out when I try to do too much at one time, and that leads to a horrible feeling of hopelessness. My relationship with Belle these days is very fragile. I think we're both worn out, and not just from one another. We're flying to Phoenix Friday to visit Scott and Maki and the girls. It will be good to get away and enjoy our grandchildren. All this mindless drivel at work has been getting to me—but I *will* get over it.

September 16, 1995

Good week! I won my point on a new writing course, and my classes are going great. I've been energized by how well things are going, but—as always—I'm waiting for the proverbial other shoe to fall. I shouldn't feel that way; I'm receiving great feedback from my colleagues about my mentoring and teaching.

When we met last Friday, I told you that I never felt more certain of myself, that I was having positive feelings about my work and self-concept. Having said that, I'm a bit unsettled, since I told the very same thing to our family doctor just before I went into a major panic last spring. Friday turned out to be a hectic day, and the weekend was a total bust, leaving me feeling empty and down.

September 21, 1995

We just got home from Phoenix, where we had a wonderful time with Scott and his family. I'm leaving again Friday to attend a wedding in Newark, then off the following Friday to Ottawa on business. *Hey, slow down*, I tell myself. I've been trying to take care of myself by begging off meetings and other things I consider nonessential.

Later: We arrived home from Newark last night. What a rough weekend! I suspect this has to do with travel fatigue as well as being trapped in the midst of a huge wedding celebration. Swimming at noon helped revive me, but I sensed that my morning class was flat, although I picked up steam for the afternoon session. At home, I lined up work to do, but was too tired to do it. Preparing to work is half the work. On the bright side, we enjoyed a wonderful visit from Melissa, our daughter, and her husband, Keith. Now I have to pack for the Ottawa trip. One part of me wishes I could stay home. On the other hand, I will be with two friends I know and admire. It's going to be just the three of us in a country chalet somewhere in Quebec province. Maybe the weekend, albeit short, will be relaxing as we plan our August workshop.

Using your suggestion, I hereby present my list of *ifs*:

If I read some term papers this afternoon, I should be more relaxed tonight. I can wait to clean up the office after the term is over. Since I'm feeling under the weather from a combination of bronchitis, physical exhaustion, and depression, I think it's better to let others know, so they won't make any erroneous inferences about my current behavior.

If I make at least some effort to participate, I will feel better and so will my family and friends.

If I take one thing at a time instead of trying to fix everything at once, I will feel a greater sense of accomplishment.

If I don't set my standards so unreasonably high that they invite disappointment, I won't be disappointed.

If I prioritize my work so I do first things first, I won't get so upset at the last moment when I don't feel I've prepared sufficiently, which is a letdown not only for me but for others.

If I'm more honest about how I'm feeling (without going to such extremes that everything sounds like a cry for pity), I can get more support and help when I need it most.

If I can distinguish the little things in life from the big things, I can avoid the panic that results when I do the wrong things at the wrong time.

If I stop berating myself about all the things I don't know and instead concentrate on teaching what I do know, I'll feel more fulfilled.

If I recall the thousands of students who have sought my counsel over the years, I'll feel better about myself.

If I accept and appreciate the dean's compliments, I'll realize what a vital part of the organization I am.

If I stop denigrating the textbooks I have written and instead realize how incredibly successful they have been, I'll feel a sense of pride and accomplishment.

If I focus more on what I *need* to do and let others handle their own problems, I'll enjoy work more and come home feeling exhilarated instead of exhausted.

If I set a time limit for using the computer at home, I can still get my work done and have more time to spend with Belle.

Promise.

October 21, 1995

Not out of the woods by any means, but I'm starting to feel better. I've increased the Serzone to 150 mg twice daily and reduced the Xanax slightly. As a result, I'm not as sleepy or dizzy during the day and I'm focusing a bit better. Still, I feel somewhat shaky about teaching and I wonder how long I can keep doing it. I feel an overwhelming obligation to my students and worry constantly that I'm not delivering. I'm even wary of asking for anonymous student feedback, for fear that I won't like what I read.

Even though days seem a bit sunnier, there is a general feeling of despair. Will I ever get organized again? Thoughts flutter in and out of my mind. It's hard to keep things in place. I put something down and spend needless time searching for it. I seem to have lost the ability to organize my thoughts and ideas. Although I can talk one on one with students comfortably, I feel shaky about relating to them in class.

My lack of confidence keeps mounting as the week wears on. I led a successful tenure and promotion committee meeting yesterday and joined friends for dinner. Belle seemed to be having a good time, too. The following morning, I awoke with an upset stomach and feelings of panic. Here we go again.

CHAPTER 5

Smart Little Devil

By the age of four, I believed I knew everything there was to know. In kindergarten, I was the only child who could read. When the teacher passed out picture books with short captions under each picture and asked us to guess what the words said, I kept raising my hand and impatiently blurting out the answer. "Jack is running," "Betty is cooking." "The dog is barking." With smartass pride, I let the teacher and my classmates know what a genius lay in their midst!

My memories take me even further back, to when I stood up in my crib and licked the maroon wallpaper with its huge, white cabbage roses. With each lick, the paper changed color and I kept on licking, thinking how much fun it was to watch things change. Mom did not appreciate her son's artistic talent at so young an age, to put it mildly.

My bedroom opened onto a large, square room with a long dining table in the middle. Around the walls sat sofas, chairs, tables, lamps, and other pieces of living room furniture. Two huge tinted photographs of bearded old men hung above the buffet. I had no idea who they were and still don't.

We lived over the corner grocery owned by Dad and his parents at Georgia Avenue and Fairmont Street, across from

Howard University in Washington DC. At a tiny table toward the back of the store, I would sit for hours, copying the signs in the store window: chuck roast 30 cents lb., veal chops 24 cents lb., chicken 19 cents lb. Even though I saw them as mirror images from inside the store, I copied them correctly and began to read and understand the words and numbers. I have since wondered if this might have been some aberrant form of dyslexia.

My frequent rages—or temper tantrums as they were called—resulted in Mom calling on Dad to discipline me. He wasn't very good at it, but he scared me to death when he sat me on a table and threatened to give me something to cry about if I didn't stop crying. That was all it took. I cannot remember what made me cry so often, and Dad never followed through on his promise to give me "something to cry about." Yet these incidents confirmed that I must have been a great disappointment to him.

Since the store and our apartment were in a black neighborhood, my only regular playmates were the children of the woman who owned a restaurant across the street. Occasionally, Baba Sarah, my paternal grandmother, would walk me to Dishie's Restaurant and sit patiently while I played with Dishie's children. Other than that, I pretty much played solo.

I wasn't aware of it then, but Mom was not happy living with her in-laws and also felt the need to move to a white neighborhood before I entered school. So in 1940, we moved to a home on North Capitol Street, where, despite enjoying the company of other children in class and in the neighborhood, I nonetheless tended to spend much of my time alone, either reading or playing imaginary games. When Mom told me to "get off my ass" and play outside, I discovered where my ass was for the first time in my life. One day, as my new friend Buddy and I were playing in our basement, he picked up one of my sister's dolls and smashed it to smithereens. As we laughed, I picked up another doll and shattered it. One by one, we trashed my sister's doll collection. Hearing the racket, my sister—Roberta—came downstairs, and for a moment, I felt extremely guilty. To my surprise, she joined the game and smashed a few dolls on her own. Mom was not amused and yelled at us to stop at once and clean up the mess. I can imagine her thinking, "Have I given birth to two juvenile delinquents?"

A few years later, while walking with Mom and Roberta to visit Baba Bella, my maternal grandmother, my legs began to ache so badly that I had to stop at a street corner and tell Mom that I was having trouble walking. The following day, a painful spinal tap at the hospital confirmed that I had been stricken with polio. This happened in 1944, years before the Salk and Sabin vaccines, during a widespread epidemic of the paralyzing disease. As I lay helpless in a ward with other polio-stricken children, I watched as nurses plunged thick wool blankets into washing machines filled with hot water, extracted the excess moisture through the wringer over the tub, and quickly wrapped the steaming blankets around our limbs. I screamed the moment the hot blankets made contact with my legs, but as the heat penetrated the skin to ease my stiff muscles, my body seemed to acclimate itself to the temperature, and I would relax. One day, as I was chatting with the girl in the next cubicle, I asked how long we had to stay in the hospital. "Well, it takes awhile to get over polio," she replied. What a stunner; no one had told me I was a polio patient. This was an early example of how my parents would hide any information they found difficult to share with me.

Home at last, I lay in bed as my Uncle Blaine, a physician, measured my legs and told us that although one leg was slightly shorter than the other, I seemed to be in excellent health. Since I would not be allowed to return to school until the spring term, I spent most of that winter looking for things to occupy my time around the house. One day, spying a thread hanging from the kitchen curtains, I had a brilliant idea: Why not light a match and burn the tiny thread off? I never suspected that the entire set of curtains would catch fire—duh—but, of course, that was precisely what happened, leaving me terrified. Our cleaning lady saved the day—and perhaps our house—by dousing the blaze with a pail of water she was using to mop the floor. As a result, my parents gave me a lecture about playing with fire, forbade me to go to the movies for two weeks, and begged the school principal to allow me to return to classes as soon as possible. I had played with fire and, theoretically at least, had been burned.

Our next-door neighbors had two daughters, who were eager to befriend my sister and me. All summer we would sit on their front porch for hours, talking and laughing as we watched people passing by on the sidewalk. Both girls seemed to know more about "life" than we did, so we were fascinated to hear some of their stories. The girls' mother was a sweet lady, but their father was a lout with a loud voice and a mean temper, and a bearer of racist remarks. Since we lived in a row house, we could hear their high-pitched fights through the thin wall separating our home from theirs. While the yelling frightened us, it was also fascinating. To hear more clearly, Mom came up with the idea of placing drinking glasses to one ear, with the other end of the glass against the wall to magnify the sound. Having been in their home, we knew it was loaded with hundreds of fragile *tchotchkes*, mostly made of china. We assumed these came from the father's "antique" shop, though Mom said it looked to her like he ran a junk shop. As we listened to the screams next door, we heard what sounded like the shattering of many of these dubious treasures. During our next visit to their home, we would eye the tables to see how many items had disappeared.

While we visited them, we worried constantly that we might knock something over and break it, so we sat as still as we could. This was a small price to pay for their friendship, such as it was. Aside from the normal growing pains of transitioning from childhood, adolescence was a fairly happy time in my life. After sixth grade, I moved on to junior high school and instantly fell in with a great bunch of kids. Junior high also marked my initial interest in writing; I somehow managed to pen a column peppered with gossip for the school newspaper. I loved my group of friends, but I felt a different sort of attraction for a tall girl named Charlotte. Charlotte was not especially beautiful, but her smarts and her bubbly laughter hooked me dead on. I guess I must have been flirting with her during those three years in junior high, but I was too young and too dense to understand my feelings. When I found out we would be moving to the suburbs after my graduation, I made some feeble effort to tell her that I cared for her, but it came out all wrong. Ultimately, we just said we hoped we'd see one another soon, but we never did.

As I reflect upon this period of my life, I realize how manic my days had been. I was the clown, the cut-up, the smartass who believed he could move mountains. My grades were as high as my moods. Then it all came crashing down.

CHAPTER 6

Seeking the Source

In an attempt to discover how I might have inherited bipolar disorder, I began examining not only my life, but also the lives of my parents and grandparents. Beyond them, the family lineage is a blur. Seeking freedom from oppression, my four Jewish grandparents emigrated from Russia to America in the early 1900s. My maternal grandfather, Joe Birnman, began his journey by deserting the Tsar's Army. A cantankerous and strongly independent thinker, Joe saw absolutely no reason why he should endure the rigors and whims of army life. The law mandating military service, as far as he was concerned, was written by a fool. When he finally had saved enough money, Joe deserted, leaving his wife and young child—my mother—and disappeared into the night. His long journey ended in Brooklyn, New York, where he worked as a carpenter building brownstones to earn enough so that he could send for my mom and my grandmother, my Baba Bella.

By the time the three-year-old Belarusian girl who was to be my mother was told that her mother had received the money for passage to America, a Bosnian Serb student had put a wrench into their plans. He had killed the Austrian Archduke Franz

Ferdinand, thus setting the stage for World War I and making it impossible for the pair to travel west through Europe.

The only choice left was to go the longer way through Asia. With their meager belongings, mother and child crossed the vast continent by train until they reached Shanghai, where they booked passage in steerage class on a cattle boat for the long voyage to San Francisco, stopping briefly in the Hawaiian Islands.

Arriving in America, and speaking only Russian and Yiddish, they boarded one train after another on their seemingly endless journey across this immense new country. After what seemed like an eternity, their train pulled into a grandiose palace, Pennsylvania Station, in New York City. Sure enough, there was my grandpa, Joe Birnman, waiting for them and holding a clothesline tied around the neck of a small dog. Mom remembers thinking: *My father must be a rich man to be able to afford a dog.* It turned out not to be his dog at all; a neighbor had asked Joe to take the mutt into the city and release him, but I'm guessing he kept the dog anyway, because for as long as I knew him, he was never without one.

Like thousands of other newly arrived Jewish immigrants, Joe had rented rooms in Brooklyn. Rents were low, the communal bathroom was at the end of the hall, and the steam heat was a luxury, even though it did not provide quite enough warmth during the cold winters.

While Mom and her family were settling into their new lives, my father was still living in Russia with his mother, my Baba Sarah. Although Sarah's husband, Samuel, had arrived in America nearly two years earlier, Sarah was in no hurry to join this meek little man, whom she hadn't wanted to marry in the first place. Her flirtatious ways and dazzling beauty had attracted the eyes of a dashing Russian Cossack, who had wined and dined his Jewish love and then abruptly abandoned her when his regiment was moved to another part of the country. Devastated, she had stubbornly refused to follow her husband to America until her parents virtually threw her out of the house with enough money for the journey.

Each spring, Baba Bella would take my mom, whom she had named Esther, out of steamy New York City to Washington DC, where they would spend a month with cousins. It was a great escape from the dingy tenements of the big city, and Mom loved the warm summer air and green vistas of the nation's capital. She called these trips "going to the country." As she matured into a young woman, she made the journey alone, and began to meet young Jewish men who were captivated by her vibrant personality as well as her beauty.

Mom ultimately met my Dad, Morris Jewler, at a Jewish Community Center dance. Whenever she told him she had to catch the train back to New York, Morris kept demanding that she stay longer and make her trips more frequent. In 1932, when she was twenty years old, they were married.

My parents, my father's parents, my sister Roberta, and I lived above the family grocery store, S. Jewler and Son. Living with her in-laws, especially the stormy Sarah Jewler, was no treat for Mom. Sarah was shocked at the naiveté of her young daughter-in-law. Taking matters into her own hands, Baba Sarah decided to raise me, leaving my mother angry and frustrated, but powerless to demand her son back. Since I was only three, I had no idea I had caused such an acrimonious split within the family. I loved spending time with Baba Sarah, who provided me with some of the most wonderful experiences of my young life, while at the same time robbing Mom of a meaningful relationship with her young son, and vice versa.

As a result, I grew up not knowing for certain who my mother was. Baba would dress me every Monday morning and feed me an early breakfast so that we could catch the Georgia Avenue trolley to downtown F Street. Once there, we'd take in the first movie showing of the day at Loew's Capitol or Warner's Earle because both offered live vaudeville in addition to a feature film. I trace my lifelong love for film and theater to those happy mornings.

After the show, she would treat me to a hot dog and a soft drink at the luncheonette counter of Lansburgh's, her favorite department store. Though I rarely saw her purchase anything, I realized she was on friendly terms with the sales clerks, particularly the lady behind the stocking counter, who always greeted me with a smile. All of this made me feel like a very special—albeit spoiled—little fellow.

But enough was enough. As I was about to enter public school, my mother insisted that we find a small home in a good school district. In our new row house, I had a large bedroom of my own and could walk to nearby Keene School. In kindergarten, I screamed with delight when, of all the Humpty Dumpty paintings in the class, my teacher chose mine to hang in the school library. "You'll have to paint it again on a large sheet of brown paper," she explained. Once I had finished painting the larger version, I called her over excitedly, anticipating praise. Instead, she unwittingly burst my bubble when she looked it over, turned to me, and said, "I think it needs another coat of paint." I couldn't understand what she meant, so I innocently asked, "What colors should I use this time?" Giggling, she said, "Why, the same ones, of course." But what I heard was, "Why the same ones, you stupid child!"

CHAPTER 7

Sarah

I suspect that the grandmother I loved so dearly, Sarah Jewler, passed the "bipolar gene" down to me.

Sarah was a self-made woman in an era when women were expected to obey their husbands. Although she had arrived in America as a young married woman in her late twenties, Sarah had left her heart forever in Ukraine.

Gay and spirited, with an impish sense of humor and a mean temper, Sarah was a Russian Jew who dared to fall in love with a Russian Orthodox Christian. That she was already married to my grandfather only made things worse, but he was thousands of miles away, working in America to save enough money to book passage for her and my then-eight-year-old father. The young and vivacious Sarah was in no hurry to join her husband; she was having too much fun.

As a young girl, Sarah worked at the small store and tearoom her parents operated in their village. She blossomed into a captivating woman with large blue eyes, high cheekbones, and a turned-up nose that belied her Jewish background. Her thick, wavy, black hair enhanced her opalescent face.

On her eighteenth birthday, her father informed her that he had chosen a husband for her. She screamed, she cajoled.

She sulked and once even collapsed, but within the year she was wedded to a man twelve years her senior—my grandfather, Samuel Jewler.

He was her exact opposite. Short, stocky, quiet, and brooding, he had a shock of red hair that covered his forehead and hung thickly over his small, sunken eyes. His hooked nose only added to her distaste for him.

She could hardly bear to look at him. Worse, his shyness caused him to stutter constantly. Sarah was miserable!

My dad was born a year after the marriage, and Samuel emigrated to America, promising to send for Sarah and the child as soon as he could afford to pay their way. Imagine her relief at their parting! She and the baby settled into her parents' tiny home, and she continued to help her sister in the family business. Just outside the village was an Army camp housing a contingent of Cossacks, the elite corps of horsemen in tsarist Russia. Due in part to the two attractive women who served them, the Cossacks frequented the tearoom regularly.

Sarah loved every moment of it. It was so like her to flirt with the rowdy young men. Although most Jews in her village feared reprisals for being too friendly with the soldiers of the tsar, she was carefree and reckless in their presence. Joining Samuel in America was hardly on her mind. Answering his lovesick letters, she always had a ready excuse for not leaving. Her mother was ill. Her father could not spare her. The child was too young to make the perilous journey. Perhaps it was inevitable that she would soon become romantically involved with one of the handsome young Cossacks. He was tall and graceful, with flashing, black gypsy eyes and a wonderful smile. Dressed in his dashing uniform, with high black boots on his long, muscular legs and the astrakhan hat perched rakishly on his thick, black hair, he was everything she desired.

With friends, they would go on horse-drawn hayrides in the Russian moonlight as balalaikas strummed gypsy love songs, or picnic in the deep forest outside the village. Her sister helped to hide her escapades from their parents. As a Jew, she would never have been allowed even to speak to a Russian, let alone enter into an affair with one.

Then it ended as quickly as it had begun. The entire regiment was ordered to quell a riot in St. Petersburg. Sarah was devastated. It took all her willpower not to follow her lover. When they met for the final time, he kissed her tenderly and presented a token of his love, a pair of emerald earrings set in a filigree band of gold and small diamonds. He asked her to think of him each time she wore them and told her he would be as close to her as the earrings were—always and forever.

Suddenly, she could not bear the thought of living without him. By the time she left for America, my father was already ten years old.

In Washington DC, Sarah pitched right in at the family grocery store. She picked up English quickly, managed the account ledgers for the store, and drove a truck to deliver orders, hefting the packed bushel baskets on her strong shoulders. She always collected 100 percent of the bill. In an era when grocers extended credit, she would have none of it.

This tough side of her vanished completely when I was in her company. Sarah busily baked breads and sweet rolls every Friday afternoon for the Sabbath. Turning the flame on her gas oven to its lowest setting, she would urge me to create a roll from leftover dough, which she would pop into the oven before kissing me goodnight. Rising at dawn, she would bathe and dress, and hurry to the kitchen to place one of her own sweet rolls into the oven, praising me for baking such a masterpiece when I scampered downstairs moments later. Small wonder that I worshipped the ground she walked on!

Approaching fifty, regally wrapped in her Persian lamb coat with matching Russian-styled hat, she would stroll imperiously, hand-in-hand with me, through downtown F Street, stopping to pose for street photographers. As Sarah helped her husband run the small grocery store, she quickly learned how to cut meat, kill chickens, and even to skin rabbits!

In her early forties, she was a remarkably beautiful woman, with the same commanding face of her youth. But now, her hair was cut short in a mannish style, most unusual for a married woman at the time. Even more unusual was her habit of smoking when no one was around. Though she hid this habit from the family, traces of cigarette ashes in her bedroom gave her away. One must realize that "decent" women simply did not smoke in those days. She wore the emerald earrings always, whether dressed for work or for an evening out—a constant reminder of her reckless youth.

Though Baba Sarah made her presence known to all around her, her husband was quiet, hard working, and, though good-natured, quite dull. Her sisters-in-law gossiped constantly about her, blaming Sarah's rebellious ways for her loveless marriage.

When I was around seven, Baba Sarah suggested that Mom take me to see the popular actor Spencer Tracy in *Dr. Jekyll and Mr. Hyde*. "I think he'll really like that movie," she explained, smiling widely. Mom thanked her and off we went. The first time Tracy transformed himself into the evil Hyde, I ran screaming to the back of the theater. Neither heaven nor earth nor Mom could make me return to my seat. Mom had little choice but to take me home as she realized that Baba was most likely laughing at how easily she had bamboozled her weak daughter-in-law, and at the expense of her cherished grandson, yet!

The following Monday, feeling triumphant about the little joke she had played on Mom, Baba took me downtown for our weekly movie and lunch. She had just purchased tickets for a film called *Tortilla Flat* when I noticed the movie poster in front of the theater, and there was the face of Spencer Tracy, who had portrayed Jekyll and Hyde. I screamed, cried, and refused to set foot in the theatre. "But this is a different picture," Baba explained. No matter—whatever she said could not convince me to risk repeating the nightmare of the previous week. It was the first time Baba had tossed an angry look at me. She appeared flustered as she argued with the cashier about a refund, but finally got her fifty cents back. We skipped lunch that day and returned home early.

In 1944, at the age of fifty-three, she was diagnosed with lung cancer. Her former strength disappeared, and eventually she was hospitalized.

Despite their differences, Mom visited the hospital every day, keeping Baba Sarah up-to-date about the customers she knew and loved and about the antics of yours truly.

Near death, she stared off into nowhere, as if recalling something from another time, another world. Touching one earring, and then the other, she softly told my mother, "They give me strength." A faraway look bloomed in her dimmed blue eyes as she recounted the tale of her Cossack lover.

"Dear Esther," she said. "We haven't always been the best of friends, but you and Jerry are all I have now. One day these earrings will belong to you, and I hope you will remember me with love and understanding each time you wear them."

CHAPTER 8

Life after Sarah

Even from the back of the chapel, I could see how ghastly the face had been made up: a peachy, powdery complexion, with hair perfectly combed and glistening with silver overtones. As I grew older, I felt that an open casket funeral seemed to be an invasion of privacy, a pagan worship of the dead, an unnecessary cruelty for family and friends. But seeing a dead person for the first time, at the age of twelve, was utterly terrifying. I had begged Mom to let me stay at home, but Grandpa Jewler had insisted that I go. After all, the body in the coffin had belonged to a woman who had raised me with love and affection, he explained.

We were escorted from the back of the chapel, already brimming with people, into a secluded room near the coffin. As I sat firmly rooted in my seat, Mom told me I should approach the coffin to say good-bye. Shaking with fear, I slowly walked toward the casket and stared for a few seconds at the ghostly face. This was not the Baba I had loved all my life, but the shell of a human on display for the benefit of her family and friends.

Following the service, we boarded the limo and headed across the city to the old Jewish cemetery. From a distance, I watched as the coffin was lowered into the earth, and then saw something that seemed totally inconsistent with the occasion. A large motorized crane was lowering a bronze vault cover over the coffin. People around me began to joke about the insanity of spending so much money on a vault to preserve the remains. Though I felt the same, I was angered by their jests and quickly moved away from them.

After Baba's death on July 4, 1947, I began preparing for my bar mitzvah, the coming-of-age celebration for Jewish youth. The required Hebrew lessons, held at a nearby synagogue an hour after public school ended, bored me to death. Our teacher was a middle-aged witch who slapped us with her ruler if we were disrespectful or made a mistake in reading or translation. Going to Hebrew school also meant not being able to participate in after-school activities. On the big day, following my recitation of the *haftarah*—a short reading from the Books of the Prophets—the rabbi shook my hand and presented me with a beautiful prayer book, which I promptly placed on a shelf at home and forgot about. While it was great to be the center of attention, the whole idea of religion did not interest me in the least. I read prayers in Hebrew that I did not understand and couldn't wait until services concluded. This attitude was something I would struggle with throughout my life until I ultimately realized that praying in a house of worship was not a prerequisite for communicating with a higher entity.

I read recently that, while religion is for those who fear hell, spirituality is for those who have been to hell and survived. Since I have been there many times, I suppose that's why I chose to join the latter group.

After my bar mitzvah ceremony, Mom set out a marvelous table of food and drink in our finished basement for our guests. Before the crowd arrived, I sneaked downstairs to see the spread and found my Aunt Sylvia rearranging many of the platters. "Leave that alone!" I yelled. "Mom put this out and you have no right to change it." Seeing the shocked look on her face, I ran up two flights, slammed my bedroom door, and threw myself on the bed in tears, after which I joined the party and reveled at the reality of being in the spotlight. In the space of less than half an hour, I had run the gauntlet from anger to misery to joy, and at the time, didn't give it a second thought.

I regretted that Baba Sarah had not lived to see what would have been a proud moment in her life as her grandson led the congregation in prayer and declared, "Today I am a man!"

Many years later, her sister-in-law, then in her nineties, spoke of my beloved grandmother as the black sheep of the family, the one who was always dallying with one man or another behind the back of my homely and unsuspecting grandfather.

Perhaps Baba Sarah wasn't as perfect as I remember her, but she will always represent the risk-taker in me, the nonconformist, the rebellious spirit who enjoys the rewards of work, but also knows how to reap the pleasures of life. Was Sarah bipolar? Exuberant and jolly, she often retreated to the privacy of her bedroom for hours. She had a mean temper, but a loving soul. She did not "fit in" with her contemporaries, who were constantly shocked and angered by her behavior. And I suspect she could care less, just as I would have.

So although I suspect that she may have passed this condition down to me, I shall be forever grateful for what she taught me: the courage to be your true self in a world where conformity is seen as a virtue, instead of the living death it so often turns out to be.

CHAPTER 9

An Awful Adolescence

The transition from adolescence to adulthood is rarely a smooth one, but in my case, it was aggravated by a flurry of tragic incidents. Was it during this period that my bipolar tendencies began to blossom in full force?

No one had fully prepared me for the death of Baba Sarah. Since I was only twelve, I was not allowed to visit her in the hospital. Instead, I would stand at the window of her ground-floor room and speak with her through the screen. The day she died, my mother—incapable of telling me the sad news—began screaming at me to turn off the music blaring from my phonograph. Even though no one explained that Baba had died, I sensed it instantly and ran from the house crying, eventually stopping in an abandoned field about two blocks away where I yelled up at God to please keep her alive. When I returned home, I found a houseful of family and friends, some of whom wept openly.

Shortly thereafter, Grandpa and Dad closed the store for good. They were losing their shirts, and Grandpa was growing old. After a brief job as a beer salesman, Dad partnered with another man to purchase a new supermarket in the growing suburb of Silver Spring, Maryland. It was 1949, the year of my junior high graduation. Although we were now living in our own home in Washington, it made sense, financially, to move closer to the store, and this would mean saying farewell to my school chums. To put it mildly, I was hysterical. "Please let me stay with Baba Bella on New Hampshire Avenue," I pleaded, "so I can be with my friends when they start Roosevelt High this fall." My plea fell on deaf ears, so during that steamy summer we moved to an apartment in Rock Creek Gardens, midway between Silver Spring and Bethesda, Maryland.

Since no three-bedroom unit was available, my parents had to settle temporarily for a two-bedroom apartment. This meant that, while Mom and Dad shared one room and my sister had the other bedroom, my bed was at the back of the dining area, where they had set up a folding screen to give me some privacy. On evenings when they had company, the noise was so loud that I had trouble sleeping, and I began wallowing in self-pity, unable to accept the fact that this was the best they could do at the time.

That summer, Aunt Bette invited Roberta and me to spend two weeks at her cottage on the South River near Annapolis. Dad dropped us off at her home one morning. As we sat waiting for her to round up her boys and finish packing, I wandered into the laundry room and began watching the spinning towels behind the glass door of her Bendix front-loading dryer. Since the towels appeared to be dry, I opened the glass door with the dryer still running and reached in to pull some towels out. Within a matter of seconds, the whirling towels had wrapped themselves tightly around my right index finger. Luckily, I had the sense to pull the plug as I felt the bone snap and screamed in pain. Aunt Bette called Dad, who left work to drive me to the hospital, where a surgeon set the broken bone. As I recall, I had little or no anesthesia and screamed for what seemed forever until the procedure was done. To allow the bone to fuse, the doctors had wrapped a plaster cast around my arm, from just below the elbow to just above the wrist. Protruding from either side of the cast was a metal wire that had been threaded through the tip of my finger. With this awkward and uncomfortable contraption on my right arm, I rode with Dad to the first day at my new alma mater, Montgomery Blair High School.

Although the cast fascinated my fellow students, I felt ashamed, which only further thwarted my desire to make friends. Since I could not take physical education courses, I spent one hour daily in the empty cafeteria (my "study hall"). The only other person there was a kooky girl who loved to chatter. It was a way to pass the time, but served only to make me feel further isolated from the majority of students.

With my cast removed, I came out of my shell and made a few friends, but I still felt like the odd guy out. Since we did not live on the school bus route, I shared a taxi each morning with a girl in the neighborhood. After school, I found that waiting for the local bus took forever, so I began to walk several miles daily down the winding, busy four-lane highway that led to our apartment.

One day, our teacher asked if I could stay after school to work on a bulletin board with a girl named Barbara. Barbara was intelligent, lovely, and vivacious, and I quickly agreed. As we were putting the board together and enjoying each other's company, a senior boy walked by and asked Barbara if she needed a ride home. As soon as she accepted and left me there alone, my elation turned to dismay. After finishing the display, I walked home, shut myself in my room, and sobbed uncontrollably, all the while wondering why this was tearing me apart. I was fourteen, and I suppose my hormones were running at full speed. Eventually, I realized we could coexist as good friends, and during our senior year, she and I were editor and managing editor, respectively, of the school newspaper, but our relationship ended there.

In eleventh grade, an observant and benevolent English teacher, impressed with my writing skills, recommended me for an elective class in journalism. I found that I loved the class, the teacher, and the other students, and enjoyed writing for and designing the school newspaper. At last, I had found some direction in life! One summer, our journalism teacher arranged for the newspaper staff to work at a real publishing house, just a stone's throw from the school. This publisher printed and distributed a national scholastic magazine, and our duties—much to our dismay—were simply to peel address labels from long sheets of paper and stick them to each magazine. This was hardly the "experience" we were anticipating, and after a few weeks we began to seek outlets for our bored, restless souls.

One day, we stuffed a smallish classmate into a folding typewriter desk, minus the typewriter, and flipped the top to seal him inside. As several office workers walked by, we sat on the desk and chatted to muffle his screams. After a few minutes, we released him from his prison. He was unharmed, but angry. Who could blame him?

By far, our biggest thrill was the discovery of what lay behind a locked door in the plant. One day, we noticed that the door had been left ajar, and a few of us bravely trotted into what we termed "forbidden territory." The room was a maze of shelves, with publications stacked high on each of them. As we examined a few of the magazines, we realized we had found the mother lode: hundreds of soft-porn magazines that we assumed the "scholastic" publishing company was selling on the side. Stuffing as many issues as possible under our shirts, we tiptoed back to our safe area and quietly closed the door. Since the girls in our group were curious about our smirking faces, we let them see the magazines. While some expressed shock, others burst out laughing. We couldn't take the magazines home, so we dumped them into a trash can. I have often wondered if anyone ever found them.

Tragedy struck again with the death of Dad, from lymphoma, in my senior year of high school. Dad had been a heavy smoker, but it would be years before anyone connected tobacco to cancer. I recall his taking the train to visit a doctor in New York regularly, carrying only a small suitcase, and returning home within a day or so. By the time he lay helpless in a hospital bed in our apartment, barely able to walk, it never occurred to me that he was dying, for Mom did not have it within her to tell Roberta and me. One afternoon, as I was driving her home, she whispered, "Dad isn't going to get well, you know." A week or so later, I heard Mom screaming and crying early in the morning, and finally realized that Dad was gone.

With strangely mixed feelings—sad at his demise, yet happy that a huge burden had been lifted from Mom—I attended the funeral with the family. The month before he died, Dad had celebrated his forty-first birthday.

Although my last two years at Montgomery Blair were rewarding, I rarely saw my classmates outside of school and was one of the few who was not dating. After our graduation ceremony, the large crowd left the stadium to change for the senior prom while I drove Mom and Roberta home.

Relatives helped set Mom up in a candy shop franchise in Silver Spring, while I began college at the University of Maryland, using a small inheritance from my grandfather for expenses. Dividing my time between classes and the shop, I began to realize I had little interest in college and wanted to learn more about the exciting world of retailing. I had been dressing the store window and display cases for Mom and had discovered I enjoyed the work and was quite good at it. College, by comparison, seemed dull and pointless.

Frankly, my first year of college was a disaster. I became extremely overprotective of Mom and eventually began telling her how to run her store. Eventually I told Mom that I was quitting college at the end of the first term.

In her typical non-confrontational way, Mom said she was sorry and hoped I would reconsider. But I was stunned when Baba Bella yelled in her thick Jewish accent, "You don't know what you're doing with your life! You're going to ruin everything!" The next day, she handed me a scrap of paper with the name and number of a girl, the granddaughter of a friend of hers, who worked on the college newspaper. I never figured out how she knew this, and, after two days of stubborn deliberation, I picked up the phone, my hands trembling, and dialed the number.

"This is Adele," a sharp female voice answered. I stammered hideously. "I, I'm J-J-Jerry J-Jewler and I'm a journalism major. Your grandmother and mine are friends, and she gave me your number. D-do you need any help on the newspaper?"

"Help?" she said. "Damn, can you get your ass over here around six tonight?"

That evening, I walked sheepishly into a dingy room of a shabby building on campus. Thanks to Baba Bella, it would change my life forever.

Then tragedy struck again. Less than a year after Dad's death, Baba Bella suddenly died of a heart attack. Now, more than ever, I felt it was my duty to help Mom, so I commuted to campus and rushed back to the store after classes to allow her some time off.

Working on the college newspaper provided the drive I needed to complete my degree. Eventually I was named managing editor of the paper and became close friends with Roger, the editor-in-chief. Our friendship lasted beyond college, took us both to Chicago for the better part of two years, and began a new chapter in my life that greatly strengthened my self-confidence.

I drank my first of many beers at one of our late-night newspaper sessions and was so drunk I had to drive home with all the windows down in the dead of winter as I sang at the top of my lungs to keep from falling asleep. Incidentally, I do not recommend this behavior. Partying became the norm for the newspaper staff; this was my circle of friends and they were very dear to me. One of the other editors, a young and apparently rather naïve female, innocently wrote two of the wildest headlines for her edition that never got into print. As managing editor of the Monday newspaper, her top story throughout the football season recounted what had happened on the playing field the previous Saturday. As I entered the commercial print shop that published our paper to finalize my Wednesday edition, the print shop gang couldn't wait to tell me what had happened that Sunday. At Saturday's game, the Maryland Terrapins, or Terps, had wasted the University of South Carolina team, the Gamecocks. Choking on his laughter, one of the typesetters told me that the young lady in question had handed them the following banner headline: *Terps Beat Cocks 21–6*. Stifling their instincts to break into raucous laughter, the boys in the shop suggested, "Aw, you can do better than that." So she changed it—to *Terps Lick Cocks 21–6*. That one got everyone laughing all over again, except for the perplexed student editor, who finally wrote the headline that appeared in Monday's edition: *Terps Kill Cocks 21–6*.

In my senior year, I received an invitation to attend a men's honor society dinner, where a select few were to be "tapped." I had to rent a tuxedo for the dinner and ceremony. After the meal, the names of the inductees were announced and my heart sank as I learned I would not receive this honor. Afterward, I drove home alone, tore off my rented monkey suit, and collapsed on the bed in utter despair. "Guess I'm a loser after all," I thought. For better or worse, I have treated such organizations and their lofty goals with disdain ever since.

The following fall, thanks to a kind mentor, I began working on a master's degree in American Civilization. Joe Phipps was my favorite journalism teacher, a larger-than-life professional who worked in radio news for a station in Washington. I was both surprised and touched by his interest in my future. Quite directly, he asked me what my plans were after graduation. I mumbled, "The Army, I guess." Joe disagreed. "You have the professional basics for journalism," he explained. "Now you need something to write about. There's a liberal arts master's program that will teach you about America's heritage—its history, philosophy, literature, and political theory. Think about it."

Joe's encouraging words turned out to be one of the early lessons I learned from numerous mentors throughout my life. For once, I felt valued. I applied and was accepted into the program.

I began classes that fall, and by the end of the following summer, I had earned my master's degree, unaware of how that parchment scroll was to affect my life. After working at several jobs that bored me crazy, I decided, at his invitation, to join Roger on a trip to Chicago, where he was planning to attend Northwestern University in suburban Evanston. We shared the driving along the Pennsylvania, Ohio, and, Indiana turnpikes, arriving in Chicago near nightfall. This was the farthest I had ever been from home and I was consumed by a strange mixture of elation and concern. One thing was certain: I never would have made such a trip on my own.

For days, I visited one employment agency after another, following leads that led to nowhere, which further reinforced my self-doubt. Just as I was about to give up and return to Washington, a woman at one of the agencies found me a job as a copywriter for the Sears and Roebuck catalog. I would be earning $89 a week. It was a small fortune, one I desperately needed, and I joyfully accepted.

Fearing that I would goof up in my new job, I reported to work at the old Sears complex on Chicago's south side and found myself assigned to the men's accessories department. For more than a year, I learned in minute detail about men's shirts, ties, underwear, socks, belts, and trousers. I remember writing about a brand of men's boxer shorts called "Armored Crotch" because they had a double layer of cloth at that strategic point. I enjoyed the company of the two other young writers in the department. Life in the windy city agreed with me; I felt free and independent for perhaps the first time in my life.

Later that year, the arrival of a draft notice abruptly terminated my Chicago days; the notice summoned me to report to my local draft board in Washington for induction and passage to Fort Jackson, South Carolina. Regretfully, I bid farewell to magical Chicago and drove back to Washington with Roger, who by now had completed his degree and was heading to New York in search of fame and fortune in the publishing business.

When I called Mom to tell of her of my impending military service, she answered with another bit of news that overwhelmed me: "Jerry, I got married yesterday to a very rich man."

I was dumbfounded. There I'd been in Chicago for nearly a year, and suddenly I discovered that I would be returning, not to our familiar apartment, but to a lavish house I had never seen. Mom had never been privy to such wealth, and she was careful to treat her new husband and his family graciously. As quickly as the marriage began, it became apparent that things were not going to work out. Mel, Mom's new husband, became obsessively controlling and Mom was ready to divorce him within months of their union. His family pleaded with her to change her mind, and she agreed, living with this unpredictable man until his death, twenty years later.

I never blamed her for her decision. The candy shop was losing money and she had nowhere else to go. But this second marriage changed not only her life, but the lives of our entire family.

— THE THERAPY JOURNALS: 1996–97 —

September 29, 1996

Recently, I had a recurrence of panic and depression symptoms similar to those in the spring of 1995. I attempted, as you suggested, to make a list of "tasks" or "stressors" and to balance them with "rewards." I did not get very far.

I had increased the Serzone to 150 mg in the morning and 225 mg at night. I plan to drop back to 150 mg this evening and see if that helps. I rely heavily on Xanax to keep me calm, both night and day. I usually feel comfortable after 4 or 5 PM. Mornings are the worst. I awaken with a small knot in my stomach that occasionally persists throughout the day, as it did today when I was reading student papers. To calm myself, I popped an extra Xanax at noon. I need some advice as to how and when to dose.

This week, *Parade* magazine had a page on National Depression Screening Day. When I read the eight signs of depression, I could answer "yes" to all of them.

I enjoy very little these days. I feel hopeless about the future. My biggest nightmare is that I still have three more years before I can retire at sixty-five. I keep telling myself I'll make it, but I don't really believe that. I constantly fear the future will be bleak because I won't have enough money to support us. I feel both worthless and superfluous. It doesn't matter what people tell me: what a good teacher I am, how conscientiously I handle situations, how I conduct meetings so fairly, and so forth. I have a hard time believing them and feel I am merely resting on my laurels.

I'm having trouble sleeping and that makes the bad mornings even worse.

Do I ever think about killing myself? It would be a selfish thing to do and would leave Belle in bad shape, financially and otherwise. On the other hand, if I died of natural causes, Belle would have a substantial amount of money and I would not be burdened with this unbearable pain. I fervently pray that I stop thinking this way.

To recap, I'm feel shaky teaching and wonder if I can keep doing it. I feel an overwhelming sense of responsibility to my students, but I have doubts about my ability to help them learn.

Perhaps the Serzone is still kicking in. Let's wait and hope. Don't think I can take any more medicine and stay alert.

October 12, 1996

Today you said, "An imbalance of 'shoulds' and 'wants' is the primary perpetuator of anxiety and depression." Then you asked me to make a list of my "shoulds" and "wants." So here goes:

I should be filled with enthusiasm about my accomplishments. *I'm not.*

I should be able to construct a workable course outline and stick to it. *I can't.*

I should be confident in the classroom. *I'm not.*

I should feel I'm making an important contribution to my college. *I don't feel that way.*

I should enjoy great satisfaction that my textbooks are used in many colleges and universities and earn substantial royalties for me. *Are the books really that good? I wonder.*

I should be more attentive to my wife's needs for affection. *I appreciate her and love her, but it is not always easy to demonstrate this.*

I shouldn't be this insecure at my age. I've accomplished much over the last twenty-five-plus years. *Yet I still think of myself as a failure.*

I should have a more organized "to do" list. *I feel as if I'm getting worse by the week. Yet I manage to have most things done on time.*

I should have time to enjoy things. *I have the time, but don't enjoy a whole lot these days.*

I'm an adult who's helped raise two successful children. I should be proud of that. *I believe I am, but I don't want them to be burdened by my problems.*

I should have a better system for organizing articles and other references. *Most of the time, I misplace things before I can use them.*

I should be finding time to use the library more to improve my courses. *I have avoided the building for years because it's a long walk uphill and I never seem to have the patience to search for data once I'm there.*

I should be an effective teacher since I've spent years studying effective teaching, conducted workshops on effective teaching, and am currently teaching the art of teaching to doctoral candidates in journalism. *So why is it that I think of myself as a phony? Students tell me otherwise, but ...*

A ray of joy: Today a favorite former student called to tell me she has a job in New York with a direct advertising agency and said that, had it not been for my class, she wouldn't have been a candidate. I felt good momentarily, and then it passed. I wish I didn't need constant confirmation of my abilities.

At 3:15 Sunday morning, my wife's eighty-nine-year-old mother called in a panic. We got her to Providence Hospital and they relieved the shortness of breath caused by her congestive heart failure with diuretics and other medications. She had an angiogram yesterday that showed she has so many blockages on one side of the heart that an angioplasty would be too great a risk. Belle felt the full impact of her mom's mortality and cried. Our daughter had driven in Sunday from Atlanta to be with us. The prognosis for mother is that she is still active, has all her faculties, and with proper treatment, should go about enjoying life as she always did. We know that death may be imminent, but she has great strength and an uncanny ability to think positively. So it has been another upsetting weekend, and with my mind focused on Belle and her mother, I did not have the time to feel sorry for myself. Is there a lesson here?

Sitting in the waiting room of the hospital, I began thinking about my childhood. My well-meaning mother filled me with *shoulds*: "You should go out and play more instead of just staying in the house reading." My father's *should* was, "You should take more interest in religion. You're faking it." My stepfather riled me with, "You should be making more money." So many *shoulds*!

Yet I remained at the hospital, not because I felt I *should*, but because I wanted to be with my wife, daughter, and ailing mother-in-law. While it was not a happy day, it was a very meaningful one for us all.

September 14, 1997

That little sprite in the back of my head persists in whispering, "Are you for real?" But the voice is rather quiet, even though I can still hear it. On my way to class, I wonder what in hell I'm supposed to do to fill two hours, and then class is great, and I have plenty of material left over. My anxiety is at its peak as I anticipate failure, but the successful outcome leaves me feeling exuberant momentarily. Praise keeps rolling in from anonymous student feedback and from our director of graduate studies, who has received good reports from the doctoral candidates in my teaching seminar. I want so much to believe all of this.

I finally have realized that, while a little bit of anxiety is a good thing, too much can be destructive. A colleague was ranting at me during a meeting I was chairing and I just looked him in the face and told him I was going to fire him from the committee. He couldn't see the humor in it. I left without feeling shaken and wrote a diplomatically worded memo to the guy, with a copy to the dean, to remind him in polite terms just what an ass he had made of himself.

I'm also learning to take things one at a time. I just agreed to be in another play and the timing isn't great. But how I love performing! At the same time, I wonder whether I will be able to maintain my high standards in the classroom, have time to grade papers, and make certain I complete the work of the tenure and promotion committee that I chair. I make up my mind to swim at least three times a week, work from home at least one day a week, arrive at the office later in the morning when possible, and still make myself available to students who need help, even though it means spending more time in the office.

October 14, 1997

Oh, boy, I thought. *Another big downer is heading my way, and I'm backstage waiting to make an entrance.* Once I was onstage, my anxiety vanished, replaced by the utter joy of performing for an audience. During fall break on Monday and Tuesday, I moderated a panel for a conference and went directly home afterward. I had spent Thursday and much of Friday with my collaborator and our editors on the next edition of our textbook. I often find it difficult to be around my coauthor. Perhaps it's my imagination working overtime, but he strikes me as always being suspicious of anything I say. What's more, he cut me off in mid-sentence several times as I was making a few points about the next edition. Still, we make a well-balanced team, and as long as we produce good stuff and make good money, I'm in for the duration.

So what in hell am I anxious about? Sure, I have plenty on my plate these days and I'm constantly afraid I'll forget something that will screw up the works for others as well as for me. On top of that, Belle has just been told she needs a pacemaker to regulate her heart rate, so it has been a stressful time for both of us.

Belle and I went to the movies over the weekend and enjoyed being out for a change. I also watched a few movies at home, read magazines, cut the grass, and walked the dog. I think I'm going to be okay for awhile.

October 28, 1997

Belle had her pacemaker installed on Friday, so things have been a bit hectic. Yet I've benefited from a reasonable amount of sleep, along with some afternoon naps to make up for awakening at 5:30 AM to get her to the hospital.

This week I read my midterm student evaluations. They are almost unanimously positive. Physical and emotional exhaustion keeps me from being as interested in classes as I normally am, but this will pass. Once again, I feel that I'm not pulling my share, but hey, I'm nearly sixty-three and still working full-time. I'm grateful that I can escape for a late morning swim at the PE Center before my afternoon class. What a great way to reduce anxiety and depression.

Belle has been a bit depressed since the pacemaker surgery, and I hope it passes soon, for her sake.

November 30, 1997

My sleep patterns haven't changed. I get sleepy after lunch and can nap easily in the afternoon if I'm home. I wonder if the Trazadone is causing the drowsiness.

My new word for the day is "contentment." That's all I ask of life. Each day need not be sunshiny and perfect as long as I'm pleased with myself. I'm weary this afternoon from pulling materials together for a workshop in early January and tying up loose ends on the first chapter of our next textbook. Enough already.

The anxiety comes and goes these days, but mainly goes. I feel I have less to fear. I'm weathering personal crises much better than before. Yet some of the old patterns keep recurring, such as the feeling that I don't fit in with any group. This week I learned that one of my students had nominated me for a teaching award and yesterday she presented it to me in front of the class. As a result, I received a congratulatory card from another student with a lovely sentiment inside. Such priceless gifts!

I recently screened a video of myself in a play and cringed. Then and there, I decided that I was not an actor. Are my medications draining me of the energy so vital to performing?

The term is almost over, but there always seems to be something to do. I'm reminding myself to be grateful that things are going well for the moment. I feel that my colleagues respect me, and I'm trying hard to leave my negative thoughts at the office when I head for home. I'm overjoyed that our son, Scott, and his family joined us for Thanksgiving, and that Melissa, our daughter, has found true love at last. It's a wonderful time.

CHAPTER 10

Army Times

Mom and I said our good-byes on the phone the night before I reported for active duty. Next morning, I joined a group of young men at the induction center and boarded a train at Union Station that evening for the five-hundred-mile ride to Columbia, South Carolina. Thinking about what the next two years of my life would bring, I barely slept all night. As the engine chugged along the tracks, bringing me closer to the American South, a place as foreign to me as Timbuktu, I began to see myself once more as a fish out of water.

What a joy and a surprise to discover that I loved nearly every moment of the next two years in Columbia and never wanted to leave.

As the train pulled into the station early on that hot June morning, one of the first things I noticed were two signs, "White" and "Colored," on the station building. In the next instant, I realized that the terminal contained two separate waiting rooms, and I thought, *God help you if you walk into the wrong one.*

A sergeant ordered all recruits to step off the train and board the waiting bus. With the temperature rising steadily, we bounced along for the better part of half an hour until we passed through the main gate of the huge Army training base.

Miraculously, I survived the eight-week basic-training course. Each morning, at the crack of dawn, we wolfed down a greasy breakfast and assembled for our daily run. As part of our field training, we were required to master the infiltration course, a physically and mentally challenging exercise involving crawling under acres of barbed wire barriers, rifle in hand, and wearing a heavy backpack as tracer bullets lit the sky above. Terrified by the idea of crawling under those bullets—even though we were assured they were blanks—I had listened carefully to the instructions. The sergeant in charge had warned us *never* to stand up in the middle of the course. If somehow we felt couldn't finish the course, he had added, we should roll over on our backs and lie completely still until told otherwise.

As I struggled to crawl under one barbed wire barricade after another, I began swallowing bits of dirt, causing me to choke and become short of breath. "Oh, hell, this is ridiculous," I thought to myself. So, following my orders to the letter, I rolled onto my back and gazed at the brilliant tracers whizzing overhead under the starry sky. Once the firing ceased, I remained frozen in place, in accordance with the sergeant's orders. For what seemed an eternity, I lay there. It was very quiet now, and suddenly the field was flooded with light. Three worried faces were staring down at me. In a quivering voice, one of the three officers said, "Son, are you all right?" To which I replied, "Yes, sir. I just choked on the dirt and ..." But I had said enough, and he yelled, "Well, get the hell up and join your company, soldier!"

As I rose to my feet, I realized I was standing in the middle of a huge empty field, with my entire company laughing hysterically from the stands at one edge. Even though I feared retribution, I thought it was pretty funny myself.

Another day, as we were practicing on the rifle range, a lieutenant ordered me to walk to the front of the range to dislodge one of the bull's-eye targets that was not dropping properly. Instead of walking down the tunnel at the side of the range, I strolled smack down the middle, putting myself in the line of fire of a dozen or more trainees. With utter panic in his voice, the young officer screamed, "Jewler, dammit, get the hell out of the line of fire!"

To say that the Army and I did not agree would be an understatement.

Eight weeks later, basic training was over, and we were given two weeks' leave before moving on to our next assignment. Returning to Washington, I realized that all the blood, sweat, and tears of basic training had transformed me, for I felt and looked healthier and cheerier than at any time in my life.

By now, Roger was working at Time-Life in Manhattan and had invited me to visit. He was also completing his MA at the prestigious Graduate School of Journalism at Columbia University.

As I waited in the cavernous reception area of his residence hall, I noticed two doors, one marked "White," the other marked "Colored."

Not again! I thought. *Not in New York City, for gosh sakes!* When Roger stepped out of the elevator, I rushed to meet him and asked immediately, "What's behind those doors?" Somewhat confused, he explained that they were laundry rooms. You did your white clothing in one room and your "coloreds" in the other. I didn't have the nerve to explain why I had asked.

Returning to the fort, I was dismayed to learn that I had scored so well on a decoding exam that I was going to be transferred to the Army's decoding school at a top security base in Alabama. What a bore, I thought. A week later, I was summoned to the personnel office, where an embarrassed enlisted man explained that, since neither of my parents were born in the United States I could not obtain the top security clearance required for the position. *What a relief,* I thought. His next words both stunned and thrilled me: "Private, exactly where would you like to work?" Imagine the United States Army letting a lowly private choose his first duty assignment!

Later that week, I began my eighteen-month stint as a writer at the Fort Jackson public information office. What a blast! Everyone in the office had at least one college degree; most had two, as I did. Eventually, I was named editor of the base newspaper, which meant I was lucky enough to spend two days wearing civilian clothes at the local print shop in town, where we put each edition to bed.

Socially, things weren't so hot. Even though I liked most of the people in the office, I still felt like the proverbial outsider. But since I knew I had two years to kill in the service, I decided to make the most of it. I followed the guys to bars, to movies, on trips to the beach, and elsewhere.

Mom and Mel flew down one weekend to visit. Since I had been dating a local girl, I asked if I could bring my folks to her parents' home. When we arrived, both sets of parents made polite small talk, and that was it. I wasn't crazy about the girl, so I made some excuse about wanting to spend time with my family, and we left without her.

The night was young and Mel was antsy. "I don't like that girl!" he shouted. "Call somebody else." That was typical Mel for you. It was around eight o'clock on a Saturday night, and I reluctantly called the only other girl whose phone number I had, assuming she would be out for the evening. When she answered and I asked if we could pick her up, she readily accepted.

And that's how I met, fell in love with, and eventually married Belle Lavisky. Belle charmed Mel, Mom, *and* me. I was fascinated to discover that Jews actually lived down South! I later learned that Charleston, South Carolina, had one of the nation's oldest Jewish congregations.

As Belle and I were falling in love, Mom would drop indiscreet hints about whether or not I was going to marry her. One day I invited Belle to ride with me to Washington. She had never traveled far from the Carolinas and Georgia, except for a trip to Chicago to visit a former boyfriend.

Later, she would admit to being completely overwhelmed when (a) we crossed the Memorial Bridge and drove around the Lincoln Memorial, (b) she spotted the Capitol dome and the Washington Monument, and (c) she stepped into the mirrored elevator in the high rise where Mom and Mel were living. "It even has a crystal chandelier," she said, as the elevator glided smoothly to the sixteenth floor.

Both Mom and Mel welcomed Belle lovingly, and the evening was going fine until Belle offered to help Mom clear the table and, in doing so, spilled a platter of roast beef and gravy on the satin upholstery of a dining room chair. In her typical non-disparaging tone, all Mom said was, "Don't worry; it's only money."

Back in Columbia, my two-year term of duty was coming to an end, and I couldn't get up my nerve to pop the big question to Belle. How would I get a job that could support both of us? What did I want to do with the rest of my life? Finally, I asked her out for dinner, determined to settle the matter once and for all. Afterward, we drove around in near silence and ended with a brief stop at the Toddle House for chocolate cream pie with coffee. As midnight approached, I kept driving because I was at a loss for words. Lost in my dilemma, I failed to realize that we had come to the end of a paved road. Next thing I knew, we were stuck in a sea of mud. Feeling like a total idiot, I cursed myself silently, helped Belle to dry ground, and walked her to the nearby home of an aunt, who stared suspiciously as she opened the door to find us muddy and muddled after midnight.

After the tow truck pulled the car from the ditch, we drove back to Belle's house and parked. Weary and feeling lightheaded, I finally whispered, "Want to get married?"

We had a beautiful wedding in Columbia, and then we made what turned out to be a huge mistake. We moved to Washington, where I found myself in a dead-end job. Our family grew to four with the births of our daughter, Melissa, and our son, Scott. The combined stress of hating my work, earning a pittance, and having to support a family was freaking me out and I was taking out my frustrations on the ones I loved most. Years later, Belle admitted that when my car pulled into the driveway every weekday afternoon, she would tell the children to hurry and clean up their toys, because she knew from experience that if I walked into a messy house, I would fly off the handle. Once, when my beautiful nine-month-old daughter began crying uncontrollably in the car, I yelled at her to shut up. When that didn't work, I slapped her face. Shocked and angered by what I had done, Belle turned to me and gave me my comeuppance: "If you do that one more time, you'll never see your daughter again." To this day, I wonder how I could have been so thoughtless, self-serving, and just plain mean.

For eight years, we lived in the Washington area, moving from one apartment to another and finally to our first home, a modest split level we could afford only because Mom gave us the down payment.

At Mom's urging, Mel found me a job as a public-relations specialist for a local radio station. It wasn't much of a job, and I was bored to death. Since the station was only minutes from our apartment, I had lunch with Belle daily. I didn't realize then that this further constricted what free time she had. Since we had only one car, she was pretty much confined to our tiny one-bedroom apartment during her first pregnancy. It wasn't easy for her to make friends or, for that matter, to go anywhere unless she caught the bus.

With much prodding on her part, I agreed to buy a second car, and we settled on a slightly used midsized sedan. It helped somewhat, but my spendthrift attitude and compulsions about keeping our home spotless continued to blight our family life. Although Belle and I loved one another, we didn't like one another very much.

During Belle's first pregnancy, the Russians began building the Berlin wall, which resulted in my being recalled to active duty with my Army reserve unit. Fortunately, I never got anywhere near Berlin, or even Europe, for that matter. Instead, I spent the next nine months at Fort Meade, Maryland, about a thirty-minute drive from our apartment.

Most of the men in our hospital unit had been activated from Ohio, Pennsylvania, New Jersey, and adjacent states to round out our Maryland-based contingent. Their wives and children were hundreds of miles away, and they were constantly drunk, depressed, and frustrated. I could hardly blame them, for I was one of the lucky ones who could drive home each night and spend a few hours and most weekends with my loving wife.

For about a month, I was assigned temporary duty at Walter Reed Army Hospital, just a stone's throw from our apartment. I worked in the registrar's office, transferring handwritten records into a new "punch tape" system. As I typed, the machine punched holes on a roll of pink paper, which would be used to record patient data. *Brave new world!* I thought.

Meanwhile, we had gone through weeks of paperwork to receive permission that would allow us to use a civilian obstetrician to deliver our child, with the Army footing the bill. Belle did not want her baby delivered at an Army hospital. As luck would have it, a month before Melissa was born, I was discharged from active duty with no medical coverage and no money to speak of. So Mom footed the cash for our daughter's birth. It was just over two hundred dollars.

Mom's second marriage brought us more grief. Because Mel's family was rich, we became the "poor relations." It was tough on me, but even tougher on Belle, and we desperately wanted to head back south.

By the second year of our marriage, I was having serious doubts about our future, and felt I had no one to turn to except Belle's dad. I poured out my anxieties to him in a letter. Here is what he sent back:

July 13, 1961
Dear Jerry,

Your very wonderful letter expressed feelings and sentiments that I had already sensed. Our feeling for you is that for a son, and that I think you also sense. You couldn't be any more one of us had you been born into our family. However, we are long on sentiment and short on demonstration, especially me. I feel very deeply but just find it difficult to say the words. However, those who are very near and dear to me know how I feel. Some have a gift for words and rely on them greatly. I don't have that gift and so my sentiments have to come through my actions. I believe these are the truer truths. Words can conceal as well as reveal.

I think I have an inkling about your feeling for Columbia. However, I think your feeling for our city is a desire for a home base, rather than one for Columbia itself. For, on analysis, Columbia is just as phony as any other place, no better and no worse. It is a peculiarly selfish world we live in and every town is Washington. The only complete honesty is in the family and in the home, and I feel that, while you have lots of relatives in Washington, you miss the feeling of home that you found here. You found it and you liked it. Ask yourself this: If Mother and I were not in Columbia, would our city mean much to you? You are very much like us in feelings and sentiments; we fight and we argue, but we also love unselfishly, and we are very close to one another.

Youth lacks patience. A few years ago, when I was so ill and financially flat, I couldn't think straight. I left Belle with Aunt Ada, and mother and I moved to Salisbury, NC. I didn't want to, but I had to make a living. Actually, I probably could have made one in Columbia, but I think I wanted to get away from my unpleasant memories, forgetting the good things I was leaving behind. I wasn't happy away from Belle, and Mother was miserable. But fate was kind and we came back, not just to Columbia, but to family. Those few months away taught me that, after forty-five years, the city itself and my so-called friends were not the things I missed and longed for. The city was just another Salisbury and my friends had their hands

63

full with their own problems. Even my in-laws, although they wished me the best, had their own problems. That is the way the world is.

Now that we have been back in Columbia for four years, I can truthfully say that these years have been the happiest in my life. My family is together again, and I was fortunate to find another job without much trouble. It was easier than I expected. Our home was not "out of this world," but it was comfortable and, well, it was "home," thanks to Mother (Don't tell her I said so, but she is a wonderful person!). These were happy years, despite a trip to the hospital with a hemorrhage, surgery, the death of my mother, and other tough times.

But there was also Belle marrying Jerry along with the other good things that came to me, including the best health I have enjoyed in thirty years. Yes, I have lots to be thankful for, even though everything looked so damned gloomy before. All I could see then was a vegetable-like existence until the finale.

Jerry, have patience and believe in your future. Things work out for the best. Remember that Mother and I love you just as much as one of our own, and we will listen to you and help you if we can. Always love Belle deeply. She is a wonderfully honest person. Have patience with her moods. There aren't many like her.

As my mother used to say, live a little every day. Enjoy what life you have to enjoy every day. And, remember, we can hear each other on the phone as often as we need to, and I know we'll all be traveling between Columbia and Washington as often as we can. God bless you.

Dad

Reading those words, I realized I had another very special mentor cheering me on.

Eight years into our marriage, we finally got our big break. After months of searching, I found a job as an advertising copywriter in Charlotte, North Carolina. From Charlotte, we moved to Greenville, South Carolina, where, for the first time in our married lives, we enjoyed three years of near-perfect bliss. We fell in with a great group of friends and for once, we agreed more or less on whom we chose to be with and how we chose to live.

Then a phone call changed our lives again. The creative director of the ad agency where I was working had been invited by the president of the student advertising club at the University of South Carolina in Columbia to address the group. Unable to accept, he turned the assignment over to me. Since I felt insecure about my ability to speak before groups, I worked furiously to design a presentation about the ad business and drove to Columbia, wondering throughout the two-hour ride how huge a flop I was going to be.

The head of the advertising department in the College of Journalism and Mass Communications greeted me effusively. After thanking me for making the trip, he escorted me on a grand tour of the college, followed by cocktails at his home and dinner at a lovely restaurant. I was getting the full star treatment, and did it ever feel good! Afterward, in a delightful state of mania, I gave a rip-roaring presentation to a large group of student ad majors, who crowded around me afterward to thank me and to ask about getting into the business. For the first time in my life, I felt special, and that felt absolutely wonderful.

The icing on the cake was an offer by the department head to join the faculty the following fall. And so the Jewlers moved once more, to what was to become our permanent home, the city where Belle and I first met and fell in love. Belle was overjoyed to be back in her hometown, and her parents were too excited for words.

In the fall of 1972, I walked nervously to my first class and introduced myself to a group of twenty advertising and public relation majors. The class was a writing laboratory in which students were to create advertising and public relations copy that we would collectively critique. It was the beginning of a career that would span nearly thirty years.

While I was deliriously happy with my new position, things were not going well at home. Belle and I quarreled often; we had totally different ideas about religion, friends, and money. One major bone of contention involved our joining a conservative synagogue. In Charlotte and Greenville, I had convinced Belle to join a reform congregation, which I preferred to the conservative liturgy I had grown up with. But Columbia was Belle's home and Beth Shalom was her family's synagogue. Frustrated with the mostly Hebrew services and what I viewed as outmoded ideas, I reluctantly agreed while making no bones about my feelings, which put still another wedge between us.

In contrast to my wobbly family life, my professional career was zooming. I taught from 1972 until my retirement in June 2000. After several months of unstructured freedom, I began to seek ways to fill the days, and found them by becoming a volunteer docent for the South Carolina State Museum, where I conduct tours for school groups to this day. More recently, I added the Richland County Public Library information desk to my volunteer agenda. Both places have brought me new friends and the pleasure of using my talents to help and to teach others.

CHAPTER 11

Mommas

One of our greatest joys in life was the fact that our mothers instantly became close friends. Moreover, they made us laugh, helped us to smooth over the rough times in our marriage, and, with their warmth and love, brought untold happiness into our lives.

Laughter, they believed, was the antidote to whatever ailed you. Often, neither was aware of her humor, such as the time Mom ran into the mother of a friend of mine and said, "I can't remember your first name, but I know it's an unusual one."

"Mom," I replied before the other woman could speak, "it's Esther, same as yours."

"What a coincidence," Mom smiled. "Well," she added, "Esther *is* an unusual name, isn't it?"

Shortly after my sister's wedding, Mom complained, "Did Roberta and Ben have to move all the way to Washington state? They could live anywhere on the east coast, even Chicago." A geographer she was not.

Belle's mom, Emma, always was extremely precise about what she wanted. In a shop one afternoon, she spotted a small "cigarette table," the perfect size for a place in her den. She asked the clerk, "This top … is it marble?" The clerk replied, "No, ma'am, it's onyx."

Mother was puzzled. "But it looks like marble. What's the difference?"

With a stare that could melt steel, the clerk answered, "Onyx is onyx and marble is marble."

"Thanks," Mother said. "That was all I wanted to know. I'll take it."

Describing a friend who impressed her because he never forgot anything, Mother commented, "He has a memory like an envelope." Turn the envelope upside down, I thought, and he would never remember anything! Was she thinking "elephants"? Of course she was.

One day, as I was driving my Mom around town, we passed a church graveyard. "You know who's buried there?" she asked. Before I could say, "Yes, I know," she answered her own question: "F. Scott Fitzgerald and his wife—Ella." Stifling a laugh, I chose not to explain that she had confused the real Mrs. Fitzgerald with the famous jazz singer. I doubt Zelda Fitzgerald could sing scat.

Mom never seemed to run out of unique expressions: "There's one of those Swedish cars, a Vulva." Trying to impress my new bride with the businessmen she knew in Washington, Mom pointed to a huge warehouse with a sign reading "George's Appliances."

"That's George Wasserman, one of our dear friends, you know." At the Diener's carpet warehouse, she remarked, "That's Mickey and Lil Diener. Wonderful couple."

Then we passed a huge warehouse belonging to Kraft Foods. "I don't know if that's Al or Morris Kraft," she said, "but we know them both."

"No, Mom," I said. "That's cheese."

When we were showing Belle's mom around the nation's capital, I mentioned that the Washington Monument had been built in two stages. "Which came first, the top or the bottom?" she inquired. When we teased her, she admitted that this was her own little joke, just like the question she had asked after seeing the monumental statue of Abraham Lincoln at the Lincoln memorial. "I never knew he had arthritis," she murmured while staring at the enormous veins in the sculpture's larger-than-life hands.

Mother had an ailment that followed her throughout her life: she passed gas frequently and loudly. It was a family joke, albeit one we treated delicately. Once, while she was babysitting her three-year-old grandniece, Mother let loose with a loud one. "What was *that*?" asked the precocious child. Without skipping a beat, Mother replied, "A lion roared!" The tyke replied, "In my house we call it a fart."

Mother actually enjoyed telling that story to her family and close friends.

At a resort, a stranger walked up to Mother. "I'm a bra salesman. Where do you buy your bras?" Thinking she could get a deal from him, she replied, "At Davison's."

"I'll hold them up for nothing," he said, leaving Mother speechless for one of the few times in her life as she hurried off in the other direction.

Mother enjoyed telling funny stories about her friends, one of whom owned a small clothing store. One morning, this woman offered a pair of dress shoes to one of her best customers. "You'll love these," she smiled sweetly.

The customer was confused. "But Ms. Fox, these two shoes don't even match one another." Without flinching, Mother's friend said, "Yes, I know. Latest thing in New York these days." Needless to say, the customer walked out and the orphan shoes stayed in the store.

Both Mom and Mother gave us much more than laughter. They also helped us value the good things in life, even in the worst of times. They made us realize that, even when things go wrong, there is always a lesson to be learned, a lesson that ultimately makes life richer, brighter, and more fulfilling. They lived by the belief that God would look after those who were faithful to his laws. On her kitchen wall, Mom hung a plaque that expressed her philosophy of life:

Go placidly amid the noise and haste, and remember what peace there may be in silence. As far as possible without surrender, be on good terms with all persons. Speak your truth quietly and clearly—and listen to others, even the dull and ignorant; they, too, have their story. Be yourself. You are a child of the universe, and whether or not it is clear to you, the universe is unfolding as it should. Therefore, be at peace with God and keep peace with your soul. With all its sham, drudgery, and broken dreams, it is still a beautiful world. Be cheerful. Strive to be happy.

Mom never could fully understand her son and daughter. Why couldn't I make "big bucks" so that Belle and I could live better? Why didn't I have more Jewish friends? Why was I so "antisocial"? Why did I resist attending synagogue services? Why did my sister, Roberta, fail to share her new life as a wife and mother more openly? In her attempt to express her concerns, she often crossed the line, as in this letter to my sister in 1960:

Dear Roberta & Ben,

Home at last and I finally finished sorting out the clothes from the trip! What a job! It was so wonderful to see you both happy and well after the initial shock of seeing the great Northwest. It sure is big, vast, and filled with tall timber. But your way of life finally grew on me and as long as you are in accord and happy, that is all that matters.

Originally, Mom had found it difficult to accept that her daughter and son-in-law were moving across the country. It's as if she were thinking, "Why leave home when the rest of your family is here?" which, ironically, may have been their reason for moving so far away. Mom's letter continues:

I hope that when you settle in your new place you will be just as happy and content then as you seem to be now. Is there anything definite yet? Let me know what develops. Ben, Mel thinks you have a lot on the ball, as he says, and that you should be successful in any position—aim high always and don't get in a rut; you will make it!

My stepfather, Mel, was a nut case who would profess his love for Mom one day and yell insults at her and our family the next. Just as Mel thought Ben had "a lot on the ball," he regarded me as someone who didn't have the guts or the know-how to make "big bucks." That hardly enhanced my self-image. *What does he know, anyway?* I'd ask myself, but it hurt.

Mom continues:

Roberta, I was delighted with your housekeeping, even though I am not used to curtain-less windows. I'd shop the dime store to make my abode more homey. I enjoyed the warmth of your friends, and finally came to the conclusion that it isn't so bad to be so far away from family.

I only hope and pray that both of you will consider bringing up your children (I hope there will be a few) in an environment of Jewish life and gracious living. It doesn't cost any more and I hope I haven't failed you in giving you a feeling of warmth and love about the Jewish faith.

The rest of the letter clearly explains that life isn't a bowl of cherries for Mom. She has the money, but none of the happiness she deserves. I felt frustrated with her situation, and with the fact that she had made her own bed and was doomed to lie in it. I wasn't angry with her, but I kept wishing she soon would inherit Mel's estate. Only then could she be free. By the time he died, years later, most of the money had gone to pay for his extended stay in a nursing home. But back to Mom's letter:

Don't concern yourself about my present way of life. It is meaningless to me, a mere formality that I go through. Yours and Jerry's happiness is my one true pleasure. I am not geared to society living, and couldn't care less. The society of the rich that I married into *doesn't hold any glamour because these people I know are miserable and have many money problems of their own. They complain about money, visit psychiatrists (as my husband does) to find peace of mind or to discover what makes them so miserable. Although Mel is fortunate to be solvent, he is constantly depressed and visits his shrink once a week at $25 an hour. How can you be normal under these circumstances? Occasionally, this doctor has asked me to see him because Mel is not communicative—brushes everything unpleasant away, even though it affects him subconsciously, and the greatest compliment the doctor gave me was that I am a normal, well-balanced human being and that Mel's family is fortunate to have me. I just go through the motions of being friendly and they do the same. I've learned my lesson through hurts and heartaches and arguments. The doctor pleaded with me to ignore them and look out for myself. It's been tough and seems selfish, but it has been my salvation.*

So you see, Roberta, I don't "have everything" as you put it. I am trying to make the most of what I have to compensate for the family and the way of life that I miss. I am old and wise enough to realize that this is not the worst. With you and Jerry going your separate ways, I was in a desperate situation, especially since business had hit rock bottom at the candy store.

Now I feel wonderful that I can at least do things for others because I have the means. I always have the memory of my mother, Baba Bella, whose heart was bigger than her pocketbook and how she yearned to give more than she could afford to. That is why I try to do what she would have done. Believe me, and I am not bragging, but from the allowance I get each week, I can help both you and Jerry, and this almost makes everything worth it.

So even though I have poured out my heart and innermost feelings to you, I am in charge of my situation and I am confident that I will have peace of mind with God's help and your understanding. Don't alienate yourself; your plans for the future and your well-being are very important to me.

Love and best regards,
Mom

When Mel had a stroke and was unable to speak or move, Mom sat with him for hours each day in the nursing home. She could not bear to let the man who had made her so miserable for so long live his final years in solitude, even though it is questionable whether he even knew she was there.

CHAPTER 12

Heartsick

One evening in 1983, Belle and I were walking through the mall when I turned and headed for a nearby bench.

"What's the matter?" she asked.

"I'm out of breath," I explained.

That week, my doctor checked my vital signs and recommended that I see a cardiologist about a "heart cath." I never had heard that term, so I asked what it entailed. "Oh, they just insert a catheter in your body and look for blockage in your coronary arteries," he explained nonchalantly.

Feeling my anxiety level rising, I asked, "And where do they insert the catheter?"

"In your groin," he answered.

"Sorry, but I can't do that," I pleaded. With a look of disdain, he replied condescendingly, "Well, if you're that scared, I'll schedule an appointment with the cardiologist who'll be doing the procedure. Maybe that will calm you down!"

Incidentally, I am no longer a patient of this doctor.

In contrast to his offhanded manner, the cardiologist presented the facts quite differently. Calmly, he walked Belle and me through the procedure. "It isn't going to hurt because the blood vessels have no nerve endings," he explained. "All you will probably feel is a shot to anesthetize the groin area so you won't feel the catheter going in. We'll snake it through a major artery until we reach the heart. Then we'll inject a dye to give us a better picture of the situation. Incidentally, the dye will feel warm, but don't worry about that. And we'll give you something intravenously to help you relax during the procedure."

It turned out that every detail of what he told me was true. Here was a physician I could trust.

Hours after the cath, the cardiologist entered my hospital room with a sketch of a human heart, on which he had marked the numerous blockages that the cath had revealed. Instead of going home that day as expected, I underwent coronary artery bypass surgery that week.

In the 1980s, coronary artery bypass grafts, or CABG, were not as common as they are today. The night before surgery, after a tech had shaved my entire body, I lay in the hospital bed wondering whether I would ever wake from the procedure. The next afternoon, hours after the surgery, I slowly began to regain consciousness. At first, I was confused and weak, and totally unprepared for the depression that quickly set in. Perhaps it was the realization that I was not immortal. Perhaps, as physicians can explain more accurately, when a heart-lung machine does your breathing during the two-to-three-hour operation, it can mess with your body chemistry, causing temporary feelings of anxiety and depression. Having been through the experience, I can appreciate more fully the ubiquitous mind and body connection.

I spent a month or so recuperating at home, and then began a cardiovascular exercise program at the hospital to help me regain my strength and stay healthy. I was put on a daily regimen of pills that I take to this day to lower my blood pressure and cholesterol. I learned that regular exercise was a must and chose to swim three times weekly at the university's indoor pool. As part of our therapy, a dietician taught us which foods to eat and which to avoid. I followed these instructions and resumed my teaching that summer, without missing a single class. With my ankles still swollen from the incisions in my legs, where the surgeons had harvested vessels for the bypasses, I sat on the desk in front of the classroom with my sneakers loosely tied, and told the class what I had been through. I wanted them to learn that it was possible to have major surgery and survive. I also hoped they'd get the point about wellness in general, particularly the fact that, the earlier you start living healthy, the greater your chances for a long and healthy life.

In late 2000, the year I retired from the university, my coronary artery vessels had closed once more, and I went through the procedure a second time. By then, coronary artery bypass grafts were more prevalent than they were seventeen years earlier, and the second procedure appeared to go more smoothly than the first. Once more, I recuperated at home, attended six weeks of cardiovascular training, and emerged as a healthy and extremely grateful human being.

The experience taught me that taking care of your mind and body can greatly improve the quality of your life, and that fatty foods, tobacco, and stress can knock you down long before your real time on earth should be over. At the time of my second surgery, I had been in therapy for depression for five years.

CHAPTER 13

Luke

I had been new at the university and eager to make friends when Luke stopped me in the lobby of our building and introduced himself. He told me about a program he chaired that was designed to help new students survive college, and invited me to sign up for the required faculty training so I could teach the "college survival course," University 101, in the fall. I followed through and taught the course annually for a number of years.

A year or so later, Luke told me he was moving to an administrative position and had gained approval to hire a co-director to manage the day-to-day workings of the course and to conduct the faculty training. I was pleased to learn that I was his first choice for this half-time position. Luke took care of everything, from negotiating a higher salary from my dean—to be split 50-50 between my college and the 101 program—to setting me up in a comfortable office with an administrative assistant. As co-director, I would teach journalism courses twice a week, work out of the 101 office twice a week, and split Fridays between the two.

Luke's charisma, combined with his skilled management and marketing savvy, led to the creation of a national conference on improving the first year of college, an event that surged in popularity annually. Following Luke's suggestions, I had been adding more structure to the USC version of the course and introducing segments that were more cognitive, or content-oriented, than the original course had required. One of my most significant contributions in that respect was a writing requirement to help students improve the quality, not only of their writing, but also of their critical thinking processes.

One day, Luke called with another brainstorm. "There isn't a single decent textbook for college success courses," he confided, "and you and I are the two who should write one." More than a year later, Luke and I signed a contract with the same publisher who handled an advertising textbook I had written a few years earlier. When our first edition was nearing completion, I learned that it would be introduced at one of the national college success conferences planned for southern California. Generously, Luke invited anyone on our staff to attend without charge. I had declined the offer since I wasn't fond of conferences and saw no need to participate for the program's sake. But now I desperately wanted to be on hand for the book's premiere.

I went to the conference, presented a program, and participated in an author's reception underwritten by the publisher. It was an unforgettable moment.

The conferences became international with the announcement of a meeting in northern England. That summer, I had applied for, and had been granted, a paid fellowship to shadow professionals in a U.S. advertising agency over the summer months. One of Luke's British cohorts suggested a marvelous compromise. Have the ad people place you in a London agency instead. Then you can make the trip north and join the conference once your fellowship is completed. I asked for, and was granted this unusual request. Belle agreed to make her first trip across the pond and join me in London the weekend before I completed my London fellowship, after which we would both travel north for the conference.

Over six glorious weeks I learned to love London, especially its theater. I was attending one musical every Saturday and several more shows during the week. On the Saturday morning after my last day at the agency, I caught the train to the airport to meet Belle and take her to my rented flat. We had a lovely weekend attending theater, dining, and seeing the sights.

When Belle asked if she could spend a few more days in London after my departure for the conference, I was surprised but happy that she felt confident enough to venture forth alone on her first trip abroad. I purchased theater tickets for her, gave her directions for the train to the conference site, and on Monday morning we kissed good-bye and I boarded the train for Newcastle-on-Tyne, site of the conference.

Arriving shortly after noon at the hotel, I checked in and scooted down to the lobby to help with conference registration. To my surprise, my colleagues demanded to know why I hadn't been there earlier in the day when they needed me. By way of explanation, I told them that no one had asked me to arrive earlier, but I was ready to pitch in. Too late, they said, and walked off in a huff.

During the conference, I conducted a session and attended others. On the last evening, we were invited to dine at an ancient castle. At dinner, I said something to my wonderful administrative assistant, who—to my utter surprise—simply glared at me and turned away. I was dumbfounded. Back in our campus office the following week, she continued to ignore me and refused to speak, so I asked her to join me in my office so that we could shake things out.

During the next fifteen minutes, she claimed that, as we were gathering in the hotel lobby that night for the dinner in the castle, I had ignored her while chatting with just about everyone else in sight. Shocked beyond belief, I tried to explain that it had not been my intent to do any such thing. My pleas of innocence fell on deaf ears, and she fled the office in tears, adding that she was never coming back. The moment she walked out, the conference manager strode into my office. "Now see what you've done?" she charged. Her words both stunned and angered me. I was trying to solve the problem and now was being accused of exacerbating it! That made me wonder whether this person had planted the whole fabrication into the ear of my assistant. Totally shaken by the incident, I told the whole sorry story to Belle that evening. As always, she knew precisely what to do. She called and explained that I was so scatterbrained on occasion that I would forget to acknowledge my own wife! "He loves you," she told the distraught woman. "Don't ruin both of your lives by doing something drastic." I was relieved the next morning when she returned to work and began speaking to me again, and blessed Belle for her acuity.

One afternoon, Luke arranged for an office retreat, to be facilitated by a psychology professor. Toward the end of the all-afternoon session, the facilitator asked us to return to our offices and "bless our work spaces." *What in hell?* I thought. As we walked from room to room, each staffer offered thanks for the privilege of working for such a wonderful program. I shuddered as we entered my office and looked blankly at the others. "I don't have much to say, because I'm not comfortable blessing my office space," I told the puzzled group. "Some folks live to work; others work to live. I happen to be in the latter group, and if I were going to bless any space, it would have to be my home. While I love my job, I happen to love my family more," I added. As we walked to the next office, one of the staff whispered in my ear, "You like to make trouble, don't you?"

"No, I don't like to make trouble," I answered. "I just have an aversion to bullshit."

Eight years after taking the job, I decided to resign and return to fulltime teaching.

CHAPTER 14

Learning from Learners

After graduating some years ago from our advertising program, Anne had become a successful graphics editor at one of the nation's most prominent daily newspapers. Her Web page, which I still receive daily, vividly illustrates her extraordinary talent as a "lifestyle photographer," as she calls herself. It reminds me of a day some years ago when I e-mailed her to congratulate her on her success, and, in passing, to remind her that she had been one of the best students in my nearly thirty years of teaching.

What I received back was an e-mail that reminded me that things had not gone so smoothly for her in college, after all. She wrote:

Professor Jewler, your memory is failing you. I was not one of your best students. In fact, I was on the verge of dropping out. Earlier that year, my brother had been killed when a car hit him. We were very close and I simply could think of nothing else but how much life he had missed. When I returned to classes, I found it almost impossible to concentrate. You must have sensed something was wrong, for you asked if we could talk. In your office, I explained everything. You expressed compassion and empathy, but quickly told me I would be wasting my life as well if I held on to those depressing thoughts. You insisted I had talents in writing and design. And twenty years later,

I know you were right. I pulled out of my depression, began living again, and finished college with a strong grade point average. Now, as graphics editor for a major national newspaper as well as proprietor of a "lifestyle photography" business, I realize that reaching for the stars can work if you push hard enough and believe in yourself.

As a high school senior, I was first chair clarinet, leader of thirty other clarinetists in my band. Then I went to college and realized I was already far behind the "real" musicians. It would be virtually impossible to catch up. Deep down, I knew I didn't have the raw talent or personal drive I'd need to get through several hours of practice every day in order to make a stab at a career as a professional musician.

Even so, my love for learning and performing difficult musical pieces didn't just disappear when I finally decided on journalism school. It was there that I met Jerry Jewler, a professor who encouraged me, even during a great personal crisis that led to near academic failure, to keep playing the clarinet. He told me that learning to balance many activities was just as important as being good at any one thing and that if I paced myself, I could achieve a great many things. In his textbook was this quote by advertising legend Leo Burnett: "When you reach for the stars, you might not quite get one, but you won't come up with a handful of mud either." It is still prominently displayed on my refrigerator. But I don't think of Leo Burnett when I see that quote; I think of Professor Jewler.

Almost two decades after college, I finally found my way back to music through my church choir. Next week, that choir will be performing in Carnegie Hall with several other choirs and a full orchestra. I'll be singing with the altos in awe of the stage on which I'll be standing, performing Mozart's Coronation Mass, grateful for the many teachers who led me there, and knowing that I will be prepared. I have learned my notes, the Latin words, the difficult rhythms over several months of hard work, all the while balancing a career, a family, and a volunteer gig as an assistant children's choir director.

Still, at the moment I first walk on that stage, I'll not be harboring fantasies of musical greatness. In my hands will be no stars, just a black music folder cradled in my palms, an appreciation for Mozart's immense talent in my allegro-beating heart, cough drop at the ready in my pocket.
And no mud.

More recently, she blogged:

The single most important thing I learned in college is that adults can have a profound impact on young people's lives. One of my goals is to mentor young people to follow their dreams and share their God-given talents and treasures. Thankfully, I am still in contact with my two favorite professors: A. Jerome Jewler, my j-school mentor and an inspirational teacher and author, and Chris Robinson, my first photography instructor. That was the most difficult "easy A" I ever received, but the one of which I am most proud.

Sadly, one of my best students never had the chance to make a name for himself. Paige was that rare combination of striking good looks, an engaging personality, and a quick mind. As a student in my advertising classes, Paige stood tall above the rest of the class. He was everything a teacher could hope for in a student: pleasant mannered, intelligent, reliable, and comfortable with people of all ages.

For the advanced creative strategy class, he was leading a small team of students in creating a public service television campaign for a statewide association. As the team worked out the strategy for the campaign, Paige would discover a way to deliver the message visually. His ideas came quickly, and they were always sound.

One cannot help but admire such a student, and I was no exception. Paige never gave any indication that he was smarter than anyone else. He was a true team player, and we spent many hours in my office chatting about life, the advertising business, and the technical and creative skills he had been developing since early adolescence. He had already written and produced a number of radio and television commercials for clients in his small hometown, and had been paid nicely for them.

How grateful I was to have a student like him, a guy who inspired not only his fellow class members, but also his professor.

Then it all went wrong. The day before the team was to present its campaign to the client, Paige stopped by to tell me he had to make a quick trip home, but would drive back during the wee hours of the morning for the 10 AM presentation. At 9:30 that morning, the rest of the student team was setting up, but Paige hadn't shown. I was puzzled, for it was highly unlike him to miss a deadline. As the client representatives arrived, we welcomed them and, our minds filled with dark thoughts, began the presentation. Even without Paige present, his work shone, and the client was impressed.

Within the hour, I received a call that shattered us all. Paige had been driving back to Columbia in the middle of the night. Short on sleep, he had dozed off at the wheel and plowed into the back of a huge freight truck. He was rushed to the Medical University of South Carolina in Charleston, where he lingered for less than two weeks before dying. He was twenty-one years old.

How could this have happened? I asked myself over and over again. How could such a promising young man be killed before he had the chance to have a successful career, marry his girlfriend, and raise a family?

At the funeral, I offered my sympathies to the family. The entire student team had driven to the little South Carolina town to pay their respects as well. As we walked out of the chapel and into the dazzling sunshine of a beautiful spring day, we stopped and had a group hug. Tears dribbling down our faces, we squeezed one another tightly, and then separated and headed for our cars.

I thought about Paige many times during the next several months. I also thought about how fragile life can be. One moment you're a shining star; in another you're gone for good.

When someone dies after a long illness, the sorrow is cushioned by the fact that he or she is no longer suffering and the survivors have had a burden lifted from them. When someone dies without warning—especially someone as young as Paige—the sorrow lasts far longer.

Even as I write this some twenty or thirty years later, I still feel the pain of that moment.

On a campus with more than fifteen thousand students, it is hardly surprising that tragedy may strike at any time. One evening, the local newscast reported that a USC female student had been found brutally murdered. Next morning during my ten o'clock class, the students filed in more quietly than usual, and just as I was to ask them to indulge in a moment of silence for the dead student, three women in the class began weeping uncontrollably. When I approached them, they revealed that, despite the fact that the victim had been a sorority sister, they did not want to miss class in order to attend the funeral. I told them to forget about class and to do what they felt was best.

Another special student and close friend lost his brother in a car accident, and his buddy rode with me to the cemetery in North Carolina to pay our respects. An effervescent freshman who took a liking to me in our University 101 class contracted leukemia during his first term and died soon after. When I visited him in the hospital, he was all smiles, as usual, and let me know what my visit meant to him. As I left the room, his parents—who happened to be acquaintances—thanked me for my kindness and friendship to their dying son.

Certainly, there were more deaths, but the passing years have gratefully erased them from memory.

CHAPTER 15

Brokenhearted

When I'd met Belle at the airport in London, I hadn't seen her in six weeks and was expecting more of a welcome than I got. She was smiling, but I sensed an undercurrent of concern in the air. When she subsequently asked if she could spend two days in London alone after I left for the conference, I purchased theatre tickets for her to see *La Cage aux Folles, Cats,* and several other shows. Though I was concerned about her remaining in London after I left, she assured me that she was fine and only needed some idea of how to use the Underground for sightseeing, shopping, and the theater. I told myself that I was imagining there was something wrong, but I was soon to discover that I'd been absolutely right.

My six weeks had dragged by, especially the first three, when I was living with the family of my "sponsor," whom I shall call Donald. Donald worked in the personnel department of the ad agency and was my escort throughout the visit. I had purchased a bottle of Kentucky bourbon in the duty-free shop in the Atlanta airport as a gift, but when I offered it to him shortly after we arrived at his home, he thanked me, set it on the bar, and told me I could have a drink of "my whiskey" whenever I wanted. He never touched it himself. It seemed the idea of an

American whiskey—or an American anything, for that matter, was somehow repugnant to him.

Donald turned out to be the stereotypical uptight Brit. Each day I would follow him as we walked to the rail station near his home, caught the train to Waterloo Station, and transferred to the Underground for the short ride to Goodge Street, just a few blocks from the ad agency.

I soon realized that few folks at the agency were prepared for my visit. They were friendly, of course, and gave me generous amounts of their time so that I could interview them, but I never managed to form any close relationships during my six weeks there. But the interviews had given me plenty to write about, so I used my time in the office to write and refine my London experience, which I would later use in classes to explain the British approach to marketing and advertising.

As agreed, I was to move into the city after the first three weeks. The agency had rented an efficiency unit on Upper Woburn Place and I eagerly awaited my freedom from the House of Donald. Once I moved, things immediately changed for the better. Whereas the weather had been typically British up to that point—chilly, gray, and rainy—the sun shone brightly on the day I moved in, and each day became sunnier than the last. On my first Sunday of freedom, I pulled on shorts and a tee shirt and headed for a London park, where I saw all shapes of folks basking in the sun's rays. Most men, slim or grossly overweight, wore only a pair of shorts and the women wore tank tops and shorts. So I pulled off my shirt and joined them to savor the lovely spring weather.

Toward the end of my stay, I rode the Underground and British Rail to Gatwick airport to meet Belle's flight. She was leaning against a counter when I first spotted her and I ran to greet her, receiving a kiss and a soft "Hi" in response. This was her first trip overseas, and I knew she would be excited, but somehow her thoughts seemed to be elsewhere.

We spent the next three days shopping, dining, and seeing Barbara Cook, one of our favorite singers, in person at the Donmar Warehouse.

The next time I saw Belle was in Newcastle-on-Tyne, the site of the conference. She had made the rail trip without incident and was waiting in our hotel room.

At the conclusion of the conference, we flew to Italy, picked up a small Volkswagen, and headed from Pisa to Florence. After spending nearly an hour trying to find our pensione, I pulled up on a sidewalk, left Belle in the car, and found the place just around the corner. We had barely settled in when Belle gave me a look that indicated something bad was coming. "I'm moving out," she said in a flat voice. I was crushed. She explained that, if she didn't take this big step immediately, she was going to fall apart. In short, my erratic moods had driven her to the breaking point (this was years before I was diagnosed as bipolar). I was astonished, ashamed, and sad all at the same time. We hugged and cried and agreed to enjoy our European outing, which indeed we did, traveling to Venice, then to Innsbruck, Austria, and winding up in Stuttgart, Germany, for our return flight home.

How could this have happened? I kept asking myself. But it was happening, and constituted the beginning of a seven-year separation. During that time, we spoke to each other on the phone at least once a day; we went out to dinner together; we saw one another and vacationed together. But we didn't live together. Belle had rented a two-bedroom apartment across town and I insisted on paying the rent and giving her money to augment her modest salary. It was not an ugly separation, nor was it a legal one, for which I was most thankful.

Nearly seven years after our separation, we learned that my mom was dying of cancer. The disease had spread quickly, and we knew of her imminent death a scant three months before it happened. I drove to Washington every weekend to be with her, and was beside her when she died. The evening before, as I tossed and turned on a sofa in the next room, I heard her cry out, "Take me, Lord." I called Belle as soon as Mom was gone and she and Melissa made plans to fly up for the funeral. In death, as in life, my mother once more had brought Belle and me together.

When I saw Belle and Melissa off at National Airport, Belle was complaining of pains in her chest, and promised she would call her doctor while I stayed in Washington for a few days to clear up loose ends, after which I planned to drive to western Virginia to conduct a scheduled workshop.

Back in Columbia, the doctors in the emergency room diagnosed Belle's pain as gallstones. Since I was in Virginia by this time, she called to tell me that the surgery would be the following morning. No need for me to rush home, she insisted, and no need to worry. This was going to be a routine operation. Belle had arranged for a friend to drive her to the hospital, and I would be home the very next day. Still, I slept restlessly that night, wishing I were with her.

The following morning, I had packed and loaded the car so that I could depart as soon as we adjourned that afternoon. In mid-morning, a woman rushed into the conference room and told me I had an emergency call. I could not believe what the voice at the end of the line was telling me: "Your wife has suffered a massive heart attack and you must get here without delay." Quickly, I made my excuses, rushed to the car, and sped off. All four hundred miles down the interstate, I could focus on nothing else. As I got hungry, I stopped at fast food joints on the road and gorged on fat-laden burgers, fries, and shakes. What did I care if I lived or not if she was not going to be with me?

When I reached Columbia, instead of going directly to the hospital, I pulled into our driveway, lugged the baggage inside the house, stripped off my sweaty clothes, and headed for the shower. I dressed, got back into the car, and drove to Providence Hospital. I cannot explain my actions except to say that I felt exhausted and could not bear to see her until I had cleaned up and felt strong enough to prepare myself for the worst.

Arriving at the hospital, I learned that, while Belle had been scheduled for gallbladder surgery, she had awakened that morning with extremely violent chest pains. Barely able to move, she had managed to crawl out of bed and yank the phone off the table to call the friend who was planning to pick her up later that morning. He sped all the way to her place, found the door unlocked, and phoned 911, screaming, "You get here at once, dammit, or this woman is going to die."

Our two grown children greeted me solemnly. Cousins had driven down from Charlotte. Local friends had joined the group. No one offered a ray of hope.

"How is she?" I asked hesitantly.

The surgeon came in and told us that, although Belle had survived the bypass operation, she had been in and out of consciousness throughout the procedure and he couldn't guarantee what she would be like when and if she awoke. A vegetable, I thought.

But Belle awoke later that night and, wondering why a tube was lodged in her throat, gestured to the nurse and pointed to her mouth. The nurse explained that she had had bypass surgery and that the tube was helping her breathe. Belle's weary eyes opened in disbelief. She must have been thinking, *What about the gallbladder operation?*

By the next day, she was fully awake and in her own private room, and we all breathed a sigh of relief. Shortly after her recuperation, she moved back in with me. But there were stipulations.

"I'd like to have a bedroom for us on the main floor, so that I don't have to walk up the stairs so often," she explained. Within two months, our junk-filled two-car garage was transformed into a large master bedroom suite with walk-in closets and a bathroom with two sinks, a whirlpool tub, and a shower stall. And Belle came home to stay.

She and I began to discuss what had gone wrong in our marriage, pledging to each other that we would try to be more understanding in the future.

Of course, there were still shaky times to come, but we were making progress.

Meanwhile, Scott, who had graduated from Clemson University with a degree in engineering, had landed an overseas assignment in Japan with Mitsubishi. One night he called from Osaka and announced he was engaged to a Japanese woman from Kobe. To say we were surprised is putting it mildly. When Scott brought Maki to the United States, we immediately realized what a fine choice he had made. They eventually settled in San Jose, California, after living in Taiwan and Singapore, and gave us two wonderful, beautiful, and talented granddaughters, Lena and Kay.

Melissa, who initially had complained about going to college, earned an undergraduate degree in management from the University of South Carolina. Her professors were so impressed with her scholarship that they urged her to go for a master's in human resources management, going so far as to help her secure an assistantship. Once she completed the degree, she worked for a number of national fast-food chains, landing eventually at Coca-Cola in Atlanta. One day, during a break in a presentation she was delivering, a man named Keith Welsh, who had a decidedly thick British accent called her aside. "You sure talk a lot," he said. "Get used to it," Melissa answered. Within the year, they were married in a festive ceremony on Hilton Head Island, South Carolina.

Both Belle and I often thank our lucky stars for such wonderful children, and for how, despite growing up in an often-unstable household, each of them achieved success in both their personal and professional lives.

Shortly after I began bipolar disorder therapy, Belle, sensing the need for help, began her therapy sessions with the same psychiatrist. Although we find it hard to come to terms on

Jerry Jewler

certain occasions, our separate therapy sessions have helped us understand why we do what we do to one another, and how we can work to change things for the better.

— THE THERAPY JOURNALS: 2008–9 —

April 6, 2008

We left home around 6 AM and boarded the 7:30 flight to Manhattan. When our nonstop flight touched down at LaGuardia shortly after 10:30, we flagged a taxi and headed for the Carnegie Deli at Fifty-fifth Street and Seventh Avenue, where we gorged on gargantuan corned beef sandwiches, slaw, and cream soda, and—stuffed to the gills—stepped into the sunshine for a walk to the theater district.

At the St. James Theatre on West Forty-fourth and Times Square, where Patti LuPone had opened in *Gypsy* earlier that spring, we joined the line already forming on the sidewalk and waited for the doors to open for the 2 PM matinee. We had spent what for us was a small fortune for two premium seats in fourth row center. As the line moved smoothly into the theatre lobby, we headed downstairs to the restrooms and then to our seats, awaiting the magical moment.

The house lights slowly darkened. The crowd became silent. And the huge orchestra onstage sounded the opening notes of the grand *Gypsy* overture.

Three hours later, as the full house was on its feet screaming bravos to Patti and the rest of the cast, I thought to myself, "This is all I want. If I never see or hear anything again, it's okay. I have just witnessed the greatest theatrical performance of the greatest musical starring the greatest performer in history!" This is what living is all about, I thought.

Reality set in once we were back at the airport and discovered that all flights at area airports had been canceled due to severe storms. A sympathetic Delta agent handed us a confirmation receipt for a flight to Atlanta at six the next morning, with a comfortable connection home. We settled down in baggage claim; the terminal had closed and security wouldn't let us in for all the money in the world.

At around 1:30 AM, we were jarred out of our slumber by sounds of people and bags. Hurrah! The airport was coming back to life, with flights landing five, six, seven hours late. At 4:30, the security guards allowed us to walk to the gate. Upgraded to business class to make up for the delay, we fell dead asleep before takeoff. Around seven, I opened my eyes and a lovely blonde attendant was asking if we would like breakfast. We were home by noon, and slept in most of the day.

July 18, 2009

Last night, as I was watching a stupid fantasy film about a parallel universe, I began to feel warm and tingly. It felt so nice that I just sat there without moving a muscle, and allowed the tranquility to course through my body. *Is this what dying feels like?* I thought. *With my heart condition, should I call 911 or try to reach my wife?* But either of those choices would involve moving, and I did not want this rapturous experience to end. Swimmer-actor Esther Williams has spoken of a similar feeling she calls "the rapture," which frequently occurs when one is underwater for long periods and forgets to breathe because the feeling is so wonderful. Unfortunately, many end up drowning. Fortunately, Esther Williams didn't.

Finally, I slowly attempted to stand. Standing made me feel more lightheaded, but I was certain I was not going to pass out. I turned off the lamp in the den and let the dog out for her evening pee. It was 8:30, and bedtime for me usually comes between ten and midnight. But all I wanted to do was get under the covers and enjoy this eerie yet fabulous sensation. Samantha scratched at the door in a minute or two and, locking us in for the night, I drifted off and wondered if I would ever awaken.

I jerked awake and stared at the clock. Exactly 11 PM. I realized that Belle was not in bed with me. Was her 7:30 meeting still going on? Concerned, I called her cell, got her voice mail, and said, "Hi, it's past 11. Where the hell are you?" and hung up.

Where the hell she was was upstairs at her computer. Her cell was lying on our bed, but I had failed to hear it ring. The real rapture was over, but its lasting effects had put me in a happy state of transcendence. Walking into the breezy morning air to fetch the paper was heaven on earth. Something good was happening, and I didn't want to try to figure it out.

July 27, 2009

Times have been rough lately. I was bored in Santa Fe last month and felt totally wiped out the one day we spent in Albuquerque, when Belle wanted to explore Old Town and I felt hot and exhausted, not to mention short of breath. I knew she was frustrated because I was having a rough day, but spending most of that day in our hotel room as I lay there without speaking was not her idea of a vacation. Nor was it mine, but I was in the doldrums and hadn't the energy or the push to lift myself out of them.

A few weeks later, Scott and his family spent five wonderful days with us. We had eaten lavishly in Santa Fe and we ate lavishly while they were there. I gained three or four pounds, which always makes me uncomfortable.

Then came the flood. Moving the fridge out to clean our laminated wood kitchen flooring, I began to see water spilling out over the floor. As the towels I stuffed in front of the fridge grew wetter and heavier, I flipped nervously through the Yellow Pages, landing on a listing under "water removal." I called the company and they were out there within the hour. When they found the source of the leak—the icemaker line had cracked under the house and was spilling it contents everywhere—I hurried outdoors to close the main water line. It was too late; our two-year-old laminated flooring was ruined.

A week and a half later, the kitchen, with its subflooring supporting our weight, still looked like a combat zone. The fridge was sitting at the opposite end of the kitchen from where it belonged, and we were eating breakfast in the dining room.

I poured out my bad vibes during our therapy session today. We discussed various reasons for my depressed state, most of which I recognized instantly: lack of time structure (time on my hands during the museum's slow summer season), loss of interest in some activities, loss of self-confidence (I was nearly shaking when I drove to Target yesterday to buy a replacement for our dead answering machine), and now the floor disaster. He advised me not to lower my daily dosage of Xanax unless I experienced major fatigue, to swim regularly to boost my energy level and lower my anxieties, and to seek anything that would help me fill my calendar. I'm seeing him again on August 27 at 9 AM and hope things will be better before then.

July 28, 2009

Today I attended a magnificent memorial service for a man I hardly knew, Ollie Johnson, with whom I served on the board of Senior Catering, a nonprofit "meals on wheels" group. I saw Ollie only at a few meetings and at a summer retreat in 2007, yet he isn't a fellow you forget easily. The speakers at the memorial, including James E. Clyburn, majority whip of the U.S. House of Representatives—who called Ollie "my closest friend"—paid one tribute after another to this wonderful human being. Ollie had died of cancer and had left his body to medical research. Hearing his close ones speak about him this afternoon, I marveled at what an exceptional person he was. Ollie worked for the South Carolina Commission on Aging and volunteered for a number of causes to aid the needy and the elderly in this state. It was typical of him at our board meetings to quickly volunteer to call his many contacts for assistance on helping Senior Catering win the contracts it needed in order to remain viable. I don't think I've ever witnessed a religious service that held my attention throughout. As I listened to the tributes, I became aware that, no matter how down I've been, I'm a pretty lucky guy and I hope folks will remember me at least half as well as they did today for Ollie.

July 29, 2009

Paid bills today and still have a strong balance in checking. Insurance reimbursement (so far) is stashed in savings, so I can find it when the bill comes due. Tanya, who is handling the water removal and restoration process, has meticulously prepared an itemized list of costs for replacing the floor for our insurance estimator. She also informed me that she's ordered the supplies and hopes things will be rolling soon. I'm very relieved and no longer feel as if the kitchen will never be the same again.

I've begun volunteering at the main branch of the Richland County Public Library and one of the major benefits is that I am more motivated to check out books. Reading has become a pleasant escape from the dour thoughts often consuming my helter-skelter brain. Belle joined Bebe and Faye at the Mousetrap last night, and may do so weekly, and that's great as far as I'm concerned. It gives her a chance to skip cooking, and an opportunity to be with friends that make her laugh, and vice versa. Granted, I'm no bundle of laughs these days.

August 2, 2009

One of the hardest things in my life these days is trying to make Belle happy. I can't express the profound guilt within me, a guilt that stems from my inability to make even the simplest small talk with her much of the time. I know she understands, but for me that isn't enough. I look to the future and see us merely existing until one of us dies. I don't want it to be that way and still have faith that our lives will improve. Some exciting event—what it is I can't even imagine—will shatter this veil of sadness and put both of us on an even keel. If only!

Tomorrow, I will be attending the Docent Sharing Interpreters lunch with my compatriots at the museum. It will be good to be around people I feel comfortable with. At two, I'm heading for the library to complete my three-hour shift at the information desk. Our kitchen is still a war zone, but we're hopeful that restoration will begin during the coming week. Maybe that will lift my spirits. I'm not concerned, for once in my life, about how much I will have to pay out of pocket for the floor repair and the new water line to the refrigerator. I just want it over and done with.

My neck, which has been bothering me these days, doesn't ache quite so much and my back also feels a bit looser, but the soreness is still there. Next Tuesday, Belle is leaving with Susan and Dee for Las Vegas and I hope she has a ball. Her eagerness to get away and have fun is evident; she made that clear to me last week and I fully support her. I'm not much of a traveler these days. We'll be going to Hilton Head Island again in October, and I shall make a conscious effort to be pleasant, feel good, drink in the excitement of being by the ocean, and be actively involved during that week.

August 4, 2009

Yesterday was a downer. I attended the museum luncheon and was glad to see my friends after so many weeks. Then I headed to the library for my shift at the information desk. This was a mildly chaotic day, since the computers on the second and third floors were down, which meant that library patrons were lining up for one of the twenty-minute computers on the main floor. We had to show them how to sign up and remind them that they were limited to twenty minutes instead of the hour they were accustomed to. Around 4 PM, we received word that everything was working for the moment, so a large number of folks headed upstairs. At five, I walked to the car and drove home to find Belle cleaning up the mess that always results when she hosts her weekly mah-jongg game. I did what I could, but she had already taken care of the heavy stuff. We usually go out for dinner when she has the game, but I was relieved when she asked if I would mind "just having a sandwich at home," and I readily accepted. The kitchen is still god-awful. The flooring was *not* delivered yesterday, as we had expected, but it did arrive this morning. I called Belle after my annual physical with Dr. Barnick and she confirmed this, but added that the guy who delivered it said something about a delay of one or more weeks to allow the floor to acclimate to the climate in the house.

We had been told earlier that this process would take only a couple of days, so I contacted Tanya about it.

The chair I purchased last week for my computer was a good investment. I saved one hundred bucks on the retail price and brought it home completely assembled. It's a Sealy Posturepedic chair, of all things, and it is so comfortable.

I told Dr. Barnick I was seeing my cardiologist next Wednesday afternoon, so he suggested doing my stress test this week at his office. There was one opening for 8 AM tomorrow morning, and I took it.

Honestly, I have been down for so long that it doesn't seem to bother me as much these days. Is that odd? Or is it simply that I have accepted my condition, considered the alternative, and concluded that this is much, much better? Samantha is moping in the upstairs hallway and that reminds me to take her outside. I think I'll do just that and trim some shrubs while she goes about her business.

August 5, 2009

Awoke around 6:15 for my 8 AM stress test. Not hungry, no headache, drove to the office and spent the next four hours going through the process. I feel good. No word from Tanya on the floor installation date and I have decided not to bug her today. Tired of the whole kitchen floor thing and will just live with it till it's repaired. Belle is feeling the same way, I think.

As I waited for my turn on the treadmill, it occurred to me that I was living in the moment for a change, and it felt so good. No worries about later today or tomorrow, or what yesterday was about, or how I would fill the rest of my week. Just happy in the moment. Can I sustain that?

August 6, 2009

It's Thursday. I left a message for Tanya today and went swimming. When I got home, Belle said she had called back to confirm that the flooring needed one to two weeks to cure. So the builder will check in next Tuesday and see if one week is sufficient. We've rounded the bend on the floor and I'm just patiently waiting for the day when our house is back in order. It will be cause for celebration!

So here I am at home again and it's only 2:30 PM and I can't think of a thing I want to do. Guess I'll start reading a new book. The car needs washing, so maybe I'll do that and let Samantha out in the back yard so she can watch me through the gate.

August 7, 2009

It's Friday again, the end of a dull week and the prelude to a so-so weekend. At least I have library duty Monday. I'm going swimming again today, even though I just swam yesterday. Belle has gone to Spencer's—her standing "date" for Friday—to have her hair done. I've printed her Las Vegas itinerary and will print her boarding passes on Monday. Her trip will be good for her, and I plan not to have my four days without her consumed by loneliness.

August 10, 2009

It's the start of a new week, and I'm determined it will be a brighter one. I'm seeing the cardiologist at 1 PM tomorrow and by that time Belle will be on her way to Las Vegas. I wish her a great time, and hope she makes good on her promise not to lose all her money. My attitude is positive this morning. Let's keep it that way.

August 12, 2009

Belle is safely in Las Vegas, and I suspect I will hear from her sometime today. Meanwhile, I've been doing some Web surfing for the new "Deadly Medicine" exhibit at the museum. I spent a good bit of time at the museum exploring it and, though I am well aware of the Holocaust, seeing those pictures and reading those words overwhelmed me with anger and sorrow. I suspect some who see it may question its validity. But I can't help but believe that the majority will view it as what it is: a horror story that has been repeated time and time again. I took a very cool whirlpool bath last night and felt comfortable.

August 14, 2009

It's a great day, for a crew has arrived to install the new subflooring. I had to put Samantha in the kennel, where she will be calmer, and so will I! If I miss picking Sam up before five, I'll just let her spend the night there.

August 26, 2009

I've risen from the depths, so to speak, and things are sunny once more. Friday, the crew completed the kitchen floor installation and we put our home back in order. I've been swimming twice already this week, and it's only Wednesday.

Tanya is coming over tomorrow so we can settle up. After all the rain, we're having a rather sunny week and that adds to my good feelings. I have an appointment for a therapy session tomorrow and will share all this with some hesitation because each time I talk about feeling great, I plunge back into the depths soon after. Wonder why.

August 29, 2009

My therapy session was uneventful the other day. Mostly, I joked about hesitating to tell him I was feeling great, since this had been a precursor to downers in the past. I left the office feeling good, and drove home to meet Tanya and settle the bill for the floor replacement. Since the insurance check was far less than actual costs, she's going to submit the final bill to my agent and hope for the best.

CHAPTER 16

Hard Times

It was late on a Saturday night. Melissa and a group of girlfriends had enjoyed a concert and were on their way to a party. In the soft glow of the loft apartment in downtown Atlanta, she had asked where the bathroom was, and had walked briskly ahead of the person who was about to turn on some lights at the far end of the huge space.

She suddenly had the sensation of falling into a seemingly bottomless, dark hole. In a state of shock, she managed to drag herself toward a stairway and slowly pull her aching body—she realized her legs were not working—until she reached a place where her screams echoed through the room. Then she passed out.

She had fallen through an abandoned elevator shaft, left unprotected during a renovation of the loft.

Belle and I were vacationing in San Francisco when Keith called. He sobbed as he recounted Melissa's horrible fall, telling us his wife—and our daughter—was in the trauma ward of Atlanta's Grady Memorial Hospital.

"She's alive and we think she's going to be okay," he managed to say. "No need to rush here. She's in very capable hands."

When your child avoids death by a narrow margin, you envision the happy little girl of thirty years ago—the girl who never used baby talk, who spoke in perfect sentences before she was three, who was an extraordinarily beautiful child with a willful personality that belied her smiling face.

The next day, we flew home and contacted Keith. He was at the hospital and wisely said, "Let me put Melissa on the phone."

She sounded like our daughter, but the voice was weaker than usual.

"Don't worry; I've had a bad accident but I'm okay. Really."

Both she and Keith suggested that we delay our visit to Atlanta until she was released from the hospital.

"You can visit in a couple of days, okay?" Melissa asked.

And we did. Arriving at their home, we found our daughter propped up in a deeply cushioned chair, her legs on a footrest.

"We're so thankful you're okay," I said.

"Well, life's a bitch and then you die."

"Nonsense," Belle answered. "You've had a wonderful life and you will continue to do so once this awful time is behind you."

And she did.

***

For nearly three years, my life was one of unspeakable despair. I spent thousands of dollars in attorney fees and settled with the plaintiffs for $10,000. All in all, the lawsuit cost me around $40,000. I'm just grateful I was able to pay it. Haunted by the fear of losing all of my savings for the comfortable retirement I had worked for all my life, I felt helpless as large sums of money quickly vanished from my bank account.

The lawsuit involved slander. This is all I feel comfortable mentioning. What I learned from the experience is that you are *not* always innocent until proven guilty. A plaintiff with money to burn—which was the case here—can persist as long as he or she can pay attorneys to fight. When it was finally over, I had all but lost faith in the American legal system. I felt degraded and deceived. I felt that money I could hardly afford to throw away was being given to the person who had made our lives so miserable. I decided then and there that life is not always fair.

At the advice of my attorney, I wrote a letter stating that I was a heart patient who had undergone quadruple bypass surgery, that I was under the care of a psychiatrist for chronic depression and anxiety attacks, which eventually were diagnosed as bipolar disorder. I shared my concern that, while my current medication had successfully eased my mental and physical burdens, I was certain that the stress of being summoned to testify in this legal action was perilous to my health. It didn't matter. I was summoned to appear before the court on charges of which I was totally innocent and I had to pay to settle it. So much for justice.

***

In the spring of 2005, we sailed from Barcelona, heading for some of the most beautiful destinations along the Mediterranean. Our twelve-day journey would end in Venice, but, as fate would have it, we never got there.

Early one morning, as we were docking at the picturesque island of Mykonos, Greece, Belle turned to me in bed and said, "I don't feel very good." When I asked what the problem was, she replied, "I don't know, but I feel so weak I don't think I can get out of bed."

I managed to get her up and took her directly to the ship's doctor. "We must get her off the ship," he told me. "She has life-threatening anemia." We were stunned, especially after hearing his full diagnosis. She had lost nearly fifty percent of her blood supply, probably due to a bleeding ulcer. "We need to get her to a clinic at once where they have the means to treat such things," he emphasized.

As Belle was carried off the ship on a gurney and driven to a small clinic on the island, I was furiously tossing all of our belongings into our four large suitcases. Mixing bras and panties with my tuxedo and ties, I just shoved until it all fit. A ship's attendant helped me wheel the baggage to the gangplank, where I was ushered to a tiny ambulance for a ride to the clinic.

Arriving there, I met three extremely polite physicians who, after examining Belle, told me that, indeed, her bleeding ulcer had dangerously diminished her blood supply, and that the only recourse was to airlift her to a hospital in Athens for proper treatment. Since she was to be transported in a tiny helicopter, along with a doctor and the pilot, I was informed that I would have to fly commercially, which added to the anxiety of a situation already fraught with uncertainty.

Waiting at the clinic to be driven to the airport for my evening flight, I was served a complimentary takeout dinner of chicken, rice, and vegetables. Before I left, one of the doctors handed me a small piece of paper with something written in Greek and also spelled phonetically, with the English translation on the other side. It said something like, "Please take me to the Hygeia Hospital at once." It was, of course, for the taxi driver who would meet me at the Athens airport.

Once there, I paid the cabbie, who generously insisted on helping me with our luggage. After a few moments of futile exchanges that seemed interminable, I was finally able to explain to the night receptionist, a sympathetic young woman who spoke nearly perfect English, that I was looking for Belle Jewler, and, miraculously, I was in her room in a matter of minutes.

"Are you okay? What have they been doing to you?" I asked anxiously.

She explained that, although she was extremely tired, she remembered everything. Once diagnosed positively with the bleeding ulcer, she had begun a series of blood transfusions along with several medications. I was told that I could sleep in the room on a pullout cot. In my exhausted state, it felt like a posh featherbed and soon both of us were sleeping soundly.

The next morning, a middle-aged woman brought me a continental breakfast, consisting of a hard roll, coffee, butter, and juice. All Belle was allowed to eat was bland food, the most appealing choice being a crème brûlée, which she has since learned to hate.

About a week later, Belle was ready to leave the hospital and we were more than eager to fly home. When I presented my Blue Cross/Blue Shield card at the business office, it was rejected by their system. Since I did not have the $14,000 to pay the hospital bill, I handed the business manager my credit card. It, too, was rejected. I was beginning to tremble. We had reserved a flight from Athens to New York, and it was time to leave for the airport.

"You don't have an American Express card?" the hospital official asked. I didn't, but ordered one the moment we were back home.

"Look," I said. "I can pay you when I get home, but I need to move cash from one account to another. I promise you I have the money." He looked dubious, so I said, "Here. Make a copy of my debit card. You'll have your cash as soon as I can get to a computer at home."

To our great relief, he reluctantly agreed to this. And so we flew from Athens to JFK International to Columbia. I paid the bill, the cruise insurance reimbursed me for my expenses, and we thanked our lucky stars that all had turned out so well.

Since then, wherever we go, I don't leave home without you know what.

CHAPTER 17

Faith in Myself

Although I am not religious in the traditional sense, I consider myself to be a highly spiritual and moral person. I count my blessings and share my concerns with some supreme being, but I choose to do this privately, without a spiritual leader or in the midst of a house of prayer. Do I question the existence of God? To be quite frank, I do not know the answer to that.

One afternoon, as I sat reading a book at home, I heard a voice. The voice said, "It's not good enough for me."

Alone in the house, I began to wonder. Was this the voice of God telling me something in his cryptic way? I have thought about that moment ever since, and wondered what it meant, or if it meant anything, or if I actually heard it—and I've concluded that I did hear it and that it did start me thinking. What was not "good enough"? Who was "me"? Eventually, this is how I interpreted the message: "Don't let anyone knock you around or take unfair advantage of you. You're better than that. You always feel you're not carrying your share of the workload. You see yourself as a hopeless failure, despite all you have achieved. Wrong! You're carrying more of your intended share, and doing a fine job."

I avoid organized religion like the plague, yet somehow find myself envious of those who find solace in it. Ever since childhood, when I sat in synagogue listening to the same Hebrew intonations week after week, and gaining little inspiration from the often-archaic English translations in the prayer book, my tolerance for any form of organized religion has been diminishing to the point where I have stopped attending services completely.

You have the freedom to believe what you wish. But for me, religion is mostly a waste of time. Pious folks attend services in synagogues, churches, mosques, and other houses of worship to hear the pastor-rabbi-minister-priest chastise them for their sins, praise them for their virtues, inspire them to do good deeds, and leave them feeling cleansed and chaste. Then many of them commit the same sins all over again.

By the time my bar mitzvah ceremony was over, I wondered what all the fuss was. My family was elated that I had done so well. I was merely glad it was over and done with.

This was the beginning of the end of my religious life. Over the years, I slipped away from the synagogue, attending only at the behest of my mother and my wife. I anxiously sat through services until I could take no more and made a hasty exit. I found excuses to take long breaks outside the building. I would frequently drive home in the middle of the service and return for the end. And when our children were grown and married, I told Belle that was it. No more services. No more sermons. No more twiddling my thumbs for two hours or more, waiting desperately for a chance to flee. At first, it was difficult for her to understand, but we ultimately reached an agreement and an understanding. Since she finds solace in the synagogue, our tradeoff was that each would do what suited us best without interfering with one another's religious beliefs. This simple decision brought a blessed calm to our lives, especially during the high-holiday season.

I'll be frank. For me, religion, for all the good it does, has been responsible for centuries of human misery as well. Consider the seemingly insoluble situation in the Middle East. Think of the Inquisition or of the exodus of the Hebrew slaves from Egypt. Think of the mistrust between some Christians and Jews. In the not-too-distant past, a Jew was mourned if he or she married outside the faith. The parents of the son or daughter who chose to marry a non-Jew considered their offspring to be dead, recited the mourner's *kaddish*, the traditional prayer for the dead, and vowed never to see or speak to their child again. These days, with mixed marriages so common, most families have become more relaxed in their attitudes, yet some strongly urge the "outsider" to convert to Judaism prior to the wedding. I'm sure the same must be true for other faiths.

We didn't rend our garments or disown our children when both of them married non-Jews. We welcomed their spouses with open arms and prayed that they had made good choices. Time has proved that they did.

One of my favorite tales of the seamier side of religion is the novel *Elmer Gantry* by Sinclair Lewis. Recently, I watched the DVD of the 1960 movie based on the book. In case you're not familiar with the story, here is a brief synopsis:

Gantry is a boorish gadget salesman whose path crosses with that of Sister Sharon, an evangelist who travels from city to city with her entourage, holding revivals in tents to restore peoples' faith in Jesus. Gantry is stricken, not only with her beauty, but also by the brilliant way in which she motivates her worshipers to donate money to "the cause." Eventually, Gantry not only joins the tent show and becomes its main attraction, but also seduces Sister Sharon. The money comes pouring in until a local prostitute recognizes Gantry and exposes him as the lowlife creature he actually is.

The antagonist in the story is a newspaper reporter who follows the caravan as it treks through the heart of the Bible belt. An intellectual and skeptic where religion is concerned, he speaks perhaps the most honest lines in the story. In doing so, he unmasks a number of fervently pious citizens in the film as fools and phonies.

It frightens me to think of how much suffering we would avoid if people stopped hating one another because of differences in religion, culture, and ethnicity.

One day, as I was conducting a tour at the museum, a young child approached me.

"Are you a Christian?" he asked.

As a Jew, I could hardly pretend to be a Christian, just for the child's sake. Besides, I was curious. Why did he ask me that? So I deflected the question with a whispered, "I can't talk about that now. Let's get on with the tour."

But he didn't forget. At tour's end, he repeated the question and this time I knew I had to tell him the truth and hope he could fathom its real meaning. But first, I asked, "Why do you want to know?"

His answer shocked me. "Because I want to see you when I go to heaven."

This reminded me of my wife's experience with a Southern Baptist lady in her cardiac rehab class. It was mid-1999 and the lady in question told Belle, "You know, if you don't accept Christ by the millennium, you're going to hell." It was stated not with anger, but as a matter of concern. While Belle's first thought was, *Well if I do, I'll look for you there,* she tossed it off as a joke and said if the woman believed that, it was okay with Belle.

But back to the boy. I slowly explained that I was not a Christian, but a Jew. His jaw dropped in disappointment and confusion. But his mother, who was chaperoning, saved the day. "Son," she explained excitedly, "he's one of God's chosen people. So of course you'll see him in heaven." A wide grin began to spread across the boy's face and he hugged me at the knees, ran to his mother, and ran back and hugged me again.

What an adorable child, I thought. And then I thought again. Why in the world would anyone teach children that only Christians are admitted beyond the pearly gates? Was heaven merely another restricted country club?

CHAPTER 18

The Best of Friends

If you are a dog owner, you know how they take over your lives, become a part of your family, and give back the love you give them in spades. On melancholy days, a dog can cheer you up simply by an expression of love and devotion. Gracie was that kind of dog. For nearly twelve years, we enjoyed her spontaneous outbursts, our blatant annoyance when our demands fell on deaf ears, and her unforgettable smile, all of which told us she was happy living with us, just as we loved living with her.

Gracie was a handsome black standard poodle. Belle named her after Gracie Allen, the distaff side of the George Burns and Gracie Allen comedy team. The real Gracie Allen was a smart and talented performer, but her persona during their skits was just the opposite. George pretended never to know what Gracie was about to say or do. That was the shtick that made their performances hysterical. Like Gracie Allen, our Gracie was equally unpredictable. "Gracie, let's go out," we would call. And Gracie would stare at us from the opposite end of the kitchen, then turn and walk the other way.

"Gracie, time for your eye drops." And Gracie would glare at us as if we were out of our minds and run in the opposite direction. If we followed her, she would slowly lead us around the entire first floor of our home, eventually planting herself near a favorite chair in the den. Once Belle or I caught hold of her collar, she would play dead, lower her head, and just dare us to use that eyedropper.

Only when one of us gently jerked at her collar and struggled to pull her head up would she allow us to apply the drops. Gracie took steroid pills to control the Addison's Disease she was born with, a condition causing progressive anemia, low blood pressure, and weakness due to inadequate secretions of adrenalin. Addison's also strikes humans—former President John F. Kennedy was stricken with this condition.

She was a gentle dog, all fifty-five pounds of her. If she sensed it was bath time, she would retreat to one of her hiding places in the house. From there, I would have to drag her to the bathroom, shut the door, remove her collar, and try to entice her to step into our stall shower. She would walk toward the shower and plant herself firmly two feet away. From that point, it became a tug of war, with Gracie finally submitting to the indignity and helping me soak her by circling the shower area so the water could reach every inch of her sleek body.

In March 2008, we arrived home from a Caribbean cruise and, fully exhausted, tumbled into bed. The day had begun with disembarkation at 9:30 AM, followed by hours in the Fort Lauderdale airport as we awaited our 4:15 flight to Atlanta, where we would connect to our final destination.

Next morning, feeling as if I had a hangover, I was fixing the coffee when the phone rang. It was Gracie's vet. We had always boarded Gracie at his hospital and I was preparing to pick her up around noon.

"Mr. Jewler, I'm afraid I have some bad news." In the scant moments before he told me she had died the previous Thursday, I was thinking, "Gracie must have injured herself."

"She was fine that morning," Dr. Gregg explained. "Took her walk outside, came in and ate her food, and walked into her cage. Later that day, we found her dead. It appears that she died

Jerry Jewler

instantly when a tumor on her spleen burst, draining her blood supply."

I chose a mass cremation instead of a private one and gave Dr. Gregg permission to dispose of her ashes. As I hung up, Belle was coming out of the shower. "I have something to tell you," I mumbled through tears. "Gracie died on Thursday." Belle cried out and ran to me. We got into bed, pulled up the covers, and held tightly to one another as we cried the whole thing out. That evening, I dragged myself to a callback for a play. A few days later, the director informed me that I didn't get the part. No matter; it wasn't important anymore.

For a week or more, I could not shake my feelings of depression. Staring blankly at the computer screen, I could think of nothing to write about. In fact, all I could muster was a feigned interest in whatever was playing on TV. Also, my vision had deteriorated to the point where I was having trouble focusing. To boot, the spring pollen or the water in the hydrotherapy pool on the ship had caused an irritation that had dulled the hearing in my left ear. My throat felt scratchy and my voice was hoarse. I occasionally stuttered, something I hadn't done in years. I was feeling very sorry for myself. Did any of this have to do with Gracie's death? Belle insisted I see our therapist. I also called the optometrist to make an appointment for a vision check. I realized that I was scheduled for a colonoscopy the next week. I was awaiting a six-month royalty check for my textbooks and was afraid that the check might not cover the large amount of cash I knew I would have to surrender to the government because I had grossly underestimated my income for the previous year.

With so many distractions, I found that my bipolar meds failed to give me enough of a boost to lift my spirits. All I could do was let it all hang out, and detach myself as much as possible from the world.

I knew I would get through this one, just as I had with previous lows. How long it would take was something I simply

114

couldn't predict. Then one day, true to form, things began to look brighter.

A few months after Gracie's death, we finally were ready for another dog, and drove to a small town upstate to find one at a poodle rescue center. The dog turned out to be, not another standard poodle, but a poodle mix named Samantha, who didn't resemble a poodle at all. Although her mother was a labradoodle—a lab-poodle mix—Sam's father was a question mark. She was heftier than a poodle, her hair was straight except for a curly fluff behind her enormous head, and her ears were silky and smaller than Gracie's. But when she charged toward me at the shelter, leapt up to kiss me on the face, and wagged her long, bushy tail wildly, I knew she had chosen us.

CHAPTER 19

A Temporary Setback

Nearly twenty years after the publication of the first edition of our textbook, Luke called one day. "Jerry, I just spoke to our publisher and they feel we need to add a third author. They suspect we're getting too old to connect with our market, and would like a qualified young woman to join the team."

I had to admit that the publisher and Luke were probably right. As a result, we added a third author, who was not only a woman, but also Luke's wife. Although she was not the younger woman we'd discussed—she was around the same age as Luke— she was well versed in the philosophy and purpose of the course, and I felt the decision to be a sound one.

With Luke's wife aboard, we began our eighth edition. During the writing and production of this edition, our relationship began to deteriorate. I attribute part of that to the unusually difficult time I was having with my bipolar medications. During this period, my therapist had begun to wean me off lithium, which he suspected was not working effectively for me anymore. We were on a tight schedule for the book, and I often found it difficult to focus my thoughts.

One day, I picked up the phone and dialed Luke's number. When he answered, he said something that both hurt and shocked me.

"You know, Jerry, since your retirement almost seven years ago, you haven't even taught the college success course, and you choose not to attend any of the conferences. I really think *this book would be better without you.*"

I was struck dumb.

I thought long and hard about what to do. Soon after our conversation, Luke informed me that our publisher was drawing up new contracts that would ultimately terminate my involvement following the next edition. With little or no support from the publisher or Luke, I signed off on the papers and tried in vain to be optimistic about the future.

But the future held a surprise. In a swift move, our publisher had merged with another major publisher and had been directed by the Federal government to divest itself of competing titles that might violate Federal anti-trust laws. Our editor revealed this during an emotional conference call and told us how sorry she was that she no longer would be working with us. She then assured us that we had nothing to worry about; a book like ours surely would be picked up by another prominent publisher, one vetted carefully by our current publisher.

And so it happened that Bedford/St. Martins became our new home, and the individuals who would be managing our book quickly arranged a face-to-face meeting with us. We were completely taken with them and thrilled with their approach to publishing.

Despite the new management, my agreement to drop out has not changed.

CHAPTER 20

Another Teaching Turn

It wasn't supposed to happen. Through a combination of medicines, a moderately busy schedule, and my volunteer work at the museum, I was as content in the fall of 2008 as I'd ever been. The only issue gnawing at me was Luke's blatant suggestion that I should phase out of the textbooks because I hadn't taught the college success course in years.

At first, I balked at this insinuation. For more than twenty years, I had worked hard with Luke to make the series a success and, by and large, it had worked. Through the grapevine, I learned that University 101 had a new director. Belle suggested this might be an opportune time to prove Luke wrong by offering to teach a section of the course that fall.

I e-mailed the new director and his response was swift and positive. We met the following week, chose a time for the class, and that was that. I insisted on not being paid the usual stipend for teaching; I wanted this to be a "donation" to help first-year students learn how to stay in college.

Armed with a hefty armload of materials, I walked to my car and drove home. This was going to be fun. Or so I thought.

At home, I began reading the requirements of the course. Since the last time I had taught it, the course had gone from pass/

fail to letter grading. Five presentations by outside sources were mandatory. When I explained that Belle and I had an unusual number of trips scheduled during the fall term, the director kindly scheduled as many of the required presentations to occur during my absences as he could.

Naturally, I wanted to use the textbook I had been working on for some twenty years. The program required the use of an in-house text containing relevant information about the University of South Carolina, plus a second book to be chosen by the instructor. Students would have to pay for both books, and ours, like many college textbooks, was not cheap. Reluctantly, I added our book to the required list.

The course also required students to complete a number of projects: a brief research paper, attendance at cultural events, analyses of newspaper articles, and more. By the time I finished the syllabus, I was overwhelmed by the amount of work I had to require of students. Still, I was determined to abide by the rules.

The first day of a college success course is pretty straightforward: you take the roll, begin matching faces with names, tell something about yourself and why you want to teach this course, and walk students through the syllabus to explain what they must do to receive a passing grade. Then you model an exercise called "lifelines" and ask the class to present their lifelines at the next meeting.

A "lifeline" is simply a visual map on a large sheet of paper of the major events of your life. As I spoke about my childhood, my successes and failures in college, my careers in advertising and teaching, and my discovery that I was bipolar, I could feel the excitement mounting inside of me. This was a "manic attack" and it was spinning out of control. I began speaking faster and louder, rushing to finish before the end of class. I felt as if I were being jet- propelled from that room and into my car. I wondered if this tension would pass; it didn't, at least not for a while.

Yet I struggled through the term and believed I had fulfilled my obligation to my students, especially when some of them personally thanked me on the last day we met. I also vowed never to teach the course again.

As I write this, I feel a sense of accomplishment at having contributed a substantial amount of new information for the ninth edition, which—according to the agreements I signed—would be my last. I also began to believe that perhaps this was the right time to let go of the project, although I would not hesitate to continue if my colleagues and our publisher changed their minds.

One of the first things Bedford/St. Martins offered me was a free trip to the conference that would mark their entry into the college success market. Over two brief days in an Orlando hotel, I gained a new sense of self-worth as conference participants and our new publishing team greeted and complimented me for what I had contributed to the book.

Returning home, I began feeling exhausted and depressed, and those dark clouds I knew all too well began gathering in my head. I managed two museum tours on Tuesday and swam on Wednesday, but my heart wasn't in any of those things, and I sensed I was on the brink of another collapse. Besides, it was mid-February and, true to form, with the spring season would come the big downer of the year.

I called our family physician with a list of complaints. Backache, nausea, exhaustion, and so forth. Was it age or was I falling apart prematurely? "Have you called your therapist?" he asked. I made a point to do so as soon as I reached home.

By Friday, I began to feel better. A light bulb went on: After experiencing hypermania at the conference, I returned home to three days of depression and physical discomfort. In a sense, I had "created" my own pain.

With newfound enthusiasm, I plunged into the planning and writing of the new edition. I ruled out any further bickering with my coauthors and made a conscious effort to be a team player. Essentially, I realized I had no basis for disapproving of myself or others.

CHAPTER 21

Adding Things Up

As the hot summer months descend upon us, I look back on my life and try hard to be prouder of what I have achieved rather than guilt-ridden about all that I sense I've failed to accomplish. After realizing that many famous people were bipolar (try googling "bipolar disorder among famous people" and you will find a long list of them), I think of my mental disorder as a mixed blessing. Again, I wonder: Could I possibly have achieved so much without it?

I once read that one way to sell a car is to take a piece of paper, draw a line down the center, and ask the prospective buyer to list all the reasons for buying a car on the left side, and all the reasons for not buying on the right. What ultimately happens is that, by the time the prospect and the salesman have compiled a huge list of positives, the prospect finds it hard to think of many negative reasons for the purchase. In looking back on my life, I can put these items in the left column:

- I was born healthy to dedicated parents.
- I was loved by my family.
- Even though I had childhood polio, it left me unharmed.

- I had a grandmother who "kicked ass" to make me stay in college. It taught me how to be an adult.
- I had a trusted best friend.
- I ultimately found the girl of my dreams and the job of my dreams.
- I have coauthored one of the best-selling textbooks in its field, in addition to an advertising text that is a best-seller after twenty-five years.
- I have two amazing and talented children, and two amazing and talented grandchildren.
- I am in relatively good health, despite my bouts with heart disease and bipolar disorder.
- And, lastly, I'm still here.

The right-hand column? I don't have the time or patience to even think about it.